HOW
TO
LEARN

In Our
Failed Education System

Will Clark

HOW TO LEARN

In Our Failed Education System

Copyright © 2010 by Will Clark

All rights reserved. No part of this book may be reproduced or copied in any form or by any means, electronic or mechanical, including photocopying or recording, or by any information storage and retrieval system, without permission, in writing, from the author.

ISBN 1450566952

Published By
Motivation Basics
P.O. Box 6327
Diamondhead, MS 39525
228-255-5019
Will01@aol.com

GOALS OF THIS BOOK

To help students learn how to learn by understanding the process and by accepting the idea that they have gifted abilities and success potential and are capable of wonderful achievements. Those wonderful achievements, however, must be earned with sincere effort and dedication to the task of learning. Society owes them nothing but opportunity to develop their success potential. Each student chooses his or her own success or failure; that choice often made from home, peer, or other cultural or natural influences and conditions.

*

To encourage parents who don't know how to help their children learn to accept that important and necessary task. It's the most important part of the education process, and cannot and should not be left as merely a teacher and education establishment task. Most teachers are dedicated to their profession, but they cannot learn for a student and should not be the focus of parents' and students' failures.

*

To analyze problems with our education system and consider ways to improve education effectiveness. Although teachers perform a great job and do a great service for our society they need a more effective environment and a more targeted goal to help accomplish their objectives even better. Presently, society has not appointed a clear education goal at which to aim their talents and efforts. Furthermore, education research indicates student success is more influenced by each individual's economic and cultural factors than by the quality of teachers or schools. Our education policy-makers continue to disregard this finding.

CONTENTS

Page

A Learning Story	5
Introduction	13
Chapter 1 What Creates Learning?	23
Chapter 2 Our Worst Education Problem	37
Chapter 3 Creating Education Effectiveness	41
Chapter 4 A Success Plan	55
Chapter 5 Ten Parenting Coaching Skills	83
Chapter 6 Twenty Student Learning Skills	103
A Success Story	143
Conclusion	157
About The Author	160
Appendix A: Index of Parenting Skills	161
Appendix B: Index of Learning Skills	162
Bibliography	163

A Basic Learning Experience

The other end of my cotton row was a long way off. Most times I couldn't even see that end because the rows curved in several places. In the Central Mississippi hill country cultivated rows were curved around the slope's contour to keep dirt from washing away during hard rains. Cotton rows followed the same curves as the heavy-duty terraces placed at certain intervals, their closeness depending on the severity of the slope. I had been down these rows many times already and, although I couldn't see the end, I knew how far it was. It was a long way, and looked forever away for a bare-foot, ten-year-old boy.

I had seen cotton rows in the flat lands of the Mississippi Delta. They were straight, but so long one couldn't see the end of those either; some as long as a mile. I wondered how one could ever get to the other end of those.

Early in the growing season rain was welcome to make the cotton seed explode, but while that happened grass and weeds usually drank first and surged well ahead of the cotton plants, selfishly trying to leave none for their later rival. At that time, in the early nineteen-fifties, herbicides were not available, especially for small-acre farmers. The only dependable herbicide was a hoe, a tool with a handle much longer than the height of most ten-year-olds. Some still exist today, most in historical museums or propped in a seldom visited corner of a hardware store. In the nineteen-fifties, and before, it was the weapon of choice to fight grass and weeds in cotton and corn fields. Special pride blossomed from those who owned one with the best shape or the sharpest edge. When I was the youngest in the field, mine was always the most dulled reject with which I had to beat grass and weeds into submission rather than cut them with a sharp edge.

Chopping cotton was long, hard, and tedious work for a ten-year-old or one of any age. Just getting to the other end of one row was challenging. That process, seemingly simple, was more complex than could be imagined by one lacking that experience. The process could even be compared to saving a new-born baby from dangerous bullies. That new, fragile plant, only three or four inches tall, often was strangled by tenacious and hard grass and weeds. Why, then, the complicated process? Hoeing (chopping) the grass too close to the cotton plant often destroyed the fragile plant. Not hoeing close enough or deep enough left determined grass continuing its death stranglehold. It was difficult not to destroy the plant when the dirt was either too hard or too soft and flaky. Too many destroyed plants left the cotton field too sparse for a profitable yield. Too much grass created the same result, with stunted cotton plants. Sixty years later I still remember that process: leave three or four plants standing in a group, each group a little more than the width of a hoe blade apart. That allowed the removal of grass from all four sides of the plant, not just two sides.

For a profitable yield, serious decisions were required with every stroke of that hoe. Even with a perfect yield, our three-acre cotton farm was unprofitable. Only three acres were authorized for my family under the acreage allotment system at that time. My friends think I'm joking when I say I was raised on a three-acre cotton patch. Although only three acres, there was always hope for a higher acreage allotment and a better yield next year. Those anticipated better years never came for small hill farmers.

My responsibility expanded when I was fourteen. Until then my great-uncle plowed the field with a hand-held plow pulled by a horse or mule. He was a share-cropper for a larger farmer, and plowed our field during his spare time. His father, my great-grandfather, had also been a share-cropper after the end of the Civil War. At fourteen, I assumed that duty. I was surprised to learn the basic task was the same as hoeing, but the responsibilities were greater. For example, the horse or mule was a living creature who required care, concern, and nourishment. The extent of that concern was often determined by the type of plow the animal had to pull, the time of day, and the time of year.

Basic preparation of the soil was performed with a plow called a middle-buster. It was a deep running plow which threw dirt from both sides to form half a new row on both sides. A pass in the center of the next old row formed the new planting row in what had been the trail the previous planting season. A turning plow had a blade on one side forming half a middle-buster which finished forming the planting row and added more dirt volume. The sweep plow was a skimming blade angled out on both sides to cut and remove weeds and grass in the trails between the raised planted rows. A side-harrow was a springy rake-like device that loosened the soil when it became too tightly compacted near the plants.

The horse or mule required more rest when pulling the deeper running plows. They also needed more water and rest during the summer months. It wasn't uncommon for horses or mules to suffer heatstroke, and even die, if they were not cared for responsibly. While following behind that horse or mule, I always knew the animal needed more rest and water than I did. I never allowed my plow animal to be jeopardized.

Just as close attention was necessary not to destroy cotton plants when hoeing, more attention was necessary when plowing. Little things became crucial and didn't permit the luxury of a wandering mind. Running the plow too shallow created an uneven and ineffective planting bed. Running it too deep was arduous for the animal. Depth was controlled by tilting the handles. Allowing the sweep plow to wander often destroyed plants on either side.

A thoughtless nudge on one of the long reins would suggest the plow animal wander into the planted row. Inattention to the plow blade often resulted in jolting to a sudden stop when hitting a stump, or stepping with bare feet onto a bed of unearthed, newly-hatched snakes. I was jolted by many hidden stumps. Fortunately, the twisting movements of a snake bed always allowed me time to jump from that danger, since the snakes were probably more startled than I, and I was quite nimble at that young age.

Those long rows weren't any shorter while following a plow. They were still from 'one end to the other.' Even when the crop was 'laid by' those rows were as long as ever, their length still seeming endless. The term 'laid by' indicated the end to hoeing and plowing, and the crop left to finish maturing, usually about mid summer, depending upon the rain. At this time we scattered dry field peas in the laid by corn field, hoping for a bountiful side crop of field peas. Thus the name 'field peas.'

Even after the field was laid by, cotton was a special case requiring constant work, and more walks down those long rows to wage war on boll weevils. They were relentless, and destroyed the hopes, dreams, and finances of many small-acreage farmers who couldn't afford more effective equipment or more insecticide to win the battle. Vaguely, I recall an arsenic-based insecticide that was very effective but was quickly removed from the market since it was determined to be a health and environmental hazard. That was after I walked those long rows many times blowing that insecticide dust from a hand-cranked blower strapped to my chest. The apparatus had two trailing ducts that blew the dusty insecticide at the cotton boll level. Certainly, I absorbed more insecticide than did the intended targets. It was so effective that common houseflies disappeared from around our house and barn for two weeks.

Picking cotton was no less arduous, but the concept of long rows was different. If the cotton yield was sparse, the other end arrived too quickly because there wasn't enough mature cotton to pick. Either rain, boll weevils, or fertilizer quality had spoiled the yield. Picking cotton in the same row for a long time was the most desirable.

Seemingly simple, picking cotton also had many potential hazards that required close attention and care. An open cotton boll became hard with spiny points when it opened to let the cotton fibre dry in the hot summer sun. Only those most experienced could pick cotton without pricking their fingers with those sharp points. Often those pricks would result in serious infections. Snakes also cooled themselves under the shade of dense cotton plants. It wasn't unusual to see one slither away when a cool area was approached. Ordinarily, moccasins and rattlesnakes would leave early, but the copperhead was always more aggressive and reluctant to give up an area. It was more practical, however, to run instead of trying to determine the snake's species. Wasp nests were another unwelcome surprise while focusing on pulling cotton from a beautiful hand-sized, prickly cotton boll.

The horses patiently waited while the vacuum tube at the cotton gin sucked the twelve hundred pounds of cotton from the wagon. That volume usually produced a cotton bale of about eight hundred pounds, the remaining four hundred pounds being cotton seed that could be sold to the gin for resale, or returned to the wagon to save for planting the next year. Value of the bale was determined after a grader examined the quality and length of the fibre. Our farm usually produced two bales, the total value of which never recovered the costs of raising the crop. That was even considering that my time in the effort was zero value, for a period of four years.

In the summer between my sophomore and junior years of high school I finally found a real job working for someone else. I delivered groceries on a bicycle for a small grocery store in New Orleans. I don't remember the name of the store, but it was on the corner of Sycamore Street and South Carrollton Avenue.

Those months, June through August, were hot and

oppressive twelve hours a day, six days a week, but that eighteen dollars a week was real money I could spend. In that job, there were only four major hazards to avoid. One was to get to my destination without spilling the groceries in the basket on front of my bike. When I did, I always had eggs in the basket. Second was to avoid the child welfare inspector. Third was not to spend all my money at the Frostop Root Beer stores trying to stay cool. Fourth was to avoid the girl, my age, who lived two houses south of the store. She indicated she wanted to be friendly, but that was something totally outside my realm of experience. I knew about cotton, not girls. When I knew she was waiting for my return, I always took the long way back to the store. I survived that summer and returned home with about thirty dollars.

During the summer between my junior and senior years, I worked for my uncle Frank in Hortense, Georgia cutting and hauling pulpwood. Although the motions were different, the process was similar to farming cotton. In cotton, the process was one row at a time. In pulpwood, it was one pine tree at a time. Looking at all the rows, or all the trees, made the task seem difficult, if not impossible. Accepting the task of processing only one row or one tree, although not pleasant at the time, allowed the concept of reasonable success to be instilled.

As with cotton farming there were many hazards to avoid, and hazards in the forest had more dangerous consequences. Our equipment consisted of three chain saws and two small pulpwood trucks.

At seventeen, I was the oldest of the three boys operating the chain saws. Although careful, I still have a large scar on my left elbow where a chain saw blade hit it from only a minor distracted moment. Fortunately for me, it tore off only a strip of skin, without any muscle or bone damage. Although becoming proficient in felling a pine tree in the intended direction, occasionally one would twist with the falling motion and move in another direction. Worse yet was the tree that wouldn't fall and instead would kick from the bottom with a sudden release. Once the tree was felled it was trimmed then cut into four-foot segments. Even the simple process of trimming the felled tree held many hidden hazards that required total focus. Sometimes the chain saw would bounce from a springy limb. Neither was it uncommon for a half-trimmed limb to release and allow the tree to fall on an out-of-place foot.

Once the trees were trimmed and cut, the five-foot pieces were loaded by hand onto the truck into a volume called a cord. If I remember correctly a cord of pulpwood was five feet high, five feet wide, and ten feet long. The truck bed was about three feet off the ground, which meant the top layer of wood was about eight feet high. The higher the layer rose, the more dangerous it became to load, by hand. Many times did I jump away to avoid a two-hundred pound piece of wood from sliding awry at the top and falling on my head. Even that simple act of stacking a cord of pulpwood required planning and care, since all the pieces were not straight and level. Those little logs had to fit together like a puzzle to be safe and stable. Inattention was an invitation to certain disaster. Even today, with all the mechanization available for workers, the forest is still a dangerous work environment.

I earned a dollar for each cord we processed. That totaled about eighteen dollars each week; three cords a day, six days a week. The fifty dollars in my pocket when I returned home to start school that fall was enough to buy a bolt-action Remington shotgun for squirrel hunting that winter. I shot one squirrel, watched it look at me as it died in agony, and never shot another. I sold that shotgun for thirty-six dollars after I graduated from high school, in 1957, to have money when I left home to join the Air Force.

Understanding goals, hazards, determination, and results from focused efforts has guided my success and happiness. I learned these common concepts apply to all positive life efforts, and it's with this background and experience that I offer them to help improve educational aspirations for those with the willingness and insight to try.

Perhaps those without gifted backgrounds or ability who refuse to allow small, natural and positive steps guide them to the end of the row will never get there. They look at the forest, not at the tree. They look at the cotton field, not the row. They only wish for success instead of seeing, accepting, and taking those little steps necessary to lead them there. Their other option is despair and failure. Personal success, including education, is a personal choice. No one, or no society, can choose it for or force it upon another person.

Unfortunately, many choose despair and failure when they refuse to accept the positive options given to us by our Creator and our country, fought for by those who sacrificed everything to form our nation, and defended by those who, still today, give their lives in service to permit those personal choices.

INTRODUCTION

So! What About Grades?

Even in an atmosphere of failure guided and perpetuated by politicians and other senior education planners, parents still can help guide their children to success. Those students endowed with good academic skills must be allowed to reach their highest potential. Just as important, students less endowed with academic interest or prowess must not be tossed aside and have their potential destroyed by elitists' education policies. They must be guided and *allowed* to achieve their maximum potential without destroying their positive dreams of success.

Every child is destined for success in some form or avenue, and that success route is not always determined by grades. Often, it's reached just by the sheer determination *to get to the end of the row*. Their dreams must not be destroyed by forcing them to drop out of school because their interests are elsewhere. If fulfillment of our individual potential is not our purpose for existence, then what else could our purpose for existence be?

Education must be redesigned to accommodate success avenues for all children, not just for the academically gifted and those blessed with strong family support. Now, too many students lack this education support environment required to provide them with the full spectrum of perceptions and perspectives needed to anticipate success. The Equal Education Opportunity Study of 1966, *The Coleman Report*, found this lack of a full family support system, not the quality of schools or the money spent per student, to be the greatest weakness in our education efforts. Still, today, most failing students and drop-outs are from one-parent or no-parent homes. Poverty or social dysfunction often guides their actions and responses. Education elitists and senior policy-makers still try to persuade society that quality of teachers and schools is the education culprit, and that the only answer is more money.

Presently, our education system is designed backwards: the purpose fits the plan, rather than the plan fitting the purpose for education. This condition is made worse since the purpose for education has not been specified by those creating the plan. The present education plan forces at least a third of our children to drop out and not have a feeling of achievement by reaching the end of the row; the one they *perceive* as reachable. And, that perception expands as the next step on the success ladder is achieved. Success is a *learned* process, not a *taught* process.

A weakness of our economic and social system might well result more from the drop-out problem than the grade problem. Currently, the cost to house criminals is greater than the cost of education in our United States of America. Welfare and other social costs also continue to consume an inordinate share of our financial resources.

Weak grades do not create criminals and perpetual welfare cases. Instead, the high drop-out rate and the despair resulting from those lost aspirations are the underlying sources of our social and educational failures; not whether a child passes a standardized and subjective test, and whether that grade is an A, B, or C.

Students

Grades are important; but perhaps not for reasons some routinely suggest. Unless a student plans a career that requires a college degree, grades alone are not necessarily important. Other than for entry into college, grades are important because they represent a student's understanding, desire and effort to learn positive habits and success patterns. These patterns are needed for everyday living. It's the success habit that's important, not grades. It's getting to the end of the row effectively that's important, not that each stroke of the hoe requires perfection.

Ordinarily, a student who tries to make his or her best grades will continue that same effort to become successful - and happy. A student who doesn't care about being his or her best in school, or anywhere, most likely will maintain that attitude in a career or in everyday relationships with other people.

Visible success patterns are represented by grades that show the results of students' efforts. A student who doesn't have enough concern and pride to care about his or her grades most likely will not have enough concern to learn how to be successful as an adult.

Regardless of the grade, sincere and positive effort must continue. If making good grades is unrealistic or impossible, the child must be given an alternative and realistic success route - and that success route must be respected by society.

Parents

The attitudes, references, examples, and involvement of parents in their children's education are the most important things that determine if their children will be successful in school and in life. This family atmosphere of feelings and influences places itself into a child's subconscious, and is identified as *culture*.

A child reared in a family led by a success culture is more likely to adopt that culture. Success is natural for that child. The child makes good grades because it's the culture to feel efforts are rewarded.

Most parents in a success culture prepared themselves for success by completing an acceptable level of education. They demonstrate good work ethics, they are courteous and respectful to each other and the child, they are as concerned with their child's future than with just 'making ends meet' between paychecks. The child knows he or she is loved and respected, and is expected to be successful because that's just the way life is.

Before admonishing a child to study harder to make good grades, and before complaining about teachers and the education system, the parent must first ask if he or she has provided the example, the care, the interest, and the leadership necessary for the child to succeed. The parent must ask, "Does our culture support our child?"

Naturally, there are exceptions to the cultural influence. Individuals also have their own personal levels of aspirations and motivation. Some people must get to the end of the row simply because it's there.

Educators

Teachers are trained and hired to *teach*. Most who remain are certainly inspired to teach. They are not trained and hired to *learn* for students. Clearly, that's an impossible task. However, in our modern, politically correct society where it's now a social norm for individuals to avoid personal responsibility, teachers are blamed most for failing students. The blame for failing students should be in a more truthful order:

First, society should blame itself for allowing parents to shift the full education responsibility to teachers. Furthermore, no one really knows if education efforts are succeeding or not because a clear purpose, or goal, for education has never been established. Is it college preparation, career preparation, social assimilation, art appreciation? Who knows? Our education system is functioning in an expensive and confused vacuum.

Second, parents should be blamed for not having a supportive, or even a forceful, education culture if necessary in their homes.

Third, students should be blamed for avoiding their personal responsibility to perform. Those refusing to perform, or who are not capable, should be placed in vocational or other special training programs until they prove they are ready to return to normal school, accepting all the expectations and restrictions. Otherwise, there should be respect toward those students who choose an honorable career route that's not guided by school grades imposed by an educational system that doesn't comprehend its clear purpose.

Fourth, school administrations should be blamed for not providing clear and positive student disciplinary support for teachers. Now, many teachers struggle to maintain discipline in their classrooms and have little time to really teach. Teachers should be allowed to teach, not forced to be baby-sitters and disciplinarians. Respect for the teacher must be paramount in the classroom. Students must understand and accept that policy, or not be allowed into the classroom until they do.

Society has made teaching a challenge too difficult for many teachers to endure. Consequently, a teacher shortage exists in many locations, making our education system even more ineffective. Most teacher complaints are about equity and the conditions under which they must function. Their complaints about pay is not merely about the amount of money, it's about the amount of money versus expectations, treatment, support, fairness, equity, and respect.

Many teachers try to teach while trying to overcome

obstacles that discourage them from accomplishing that task. In many public schools a teacher's time is more consumed with trying to maintain discipline and order, and trying to comply with other socially-engineered demands not related to education, than on teaching.

Now, in runaway frequency teachers are being graded, judged, and evaluated by grades their students make on national tests. Good teachers are often criticized and vilified when their students make low grades on those tests, even if they are effective. Teachers are easy targets.

Serious studies prove that education effectiveness of a child is more often determined by the family and demographic culture of the student than by the school or teacher. In some districts the teacher who helps half the students achieve a passing grade is as effective as one who helps ninety percent of the students achieve a passing grade in another district.

Is Our Education System Working?

Why doesn't our education system work to perform at its highest expected level or to insure each student is prepared with life's coping skills? Our education system doesn't do what society expects because it's designed *backwards*. The education system has designed itself before society has determined the purpose for education. This is the first of three major weaknesses in our education system.

Is the purpose for education:

Social integration?

                                Basic literacy?

College preparation?

Job preparation?
Cultural assimilation?
Racial integration?
To create jobs for educators?

Is there a definitive purpose for education? Perhaps not. Perhaps the purpose for education remains transient and designs itself with little or no conscious thought or good effort by those assigned the task of educating. Society acquiesces to the purpose for education, it doesn't plan, and the purpose seems to trail the need by five to ten years.

For example, during the massive immigration to the United States in the early 1900s education's focus turned to assimilation of new arrivals to insure they shared social norms and expectations with those our society considered important at that time, which even included religious inclinations. This was after the need to insure a homogeneous society was recognized.

Another example occurred in the early 1960s. The focus at that time was on space and engineering. The U.S. was behind in the space race and the emphasis suddenly increased to specialized academic training, especially engineering and mathematics. Other areas of education were considered outcasts and inconsequential. Vocational education became an unbearable stigma on those who wanted a vocation instead of an advanced academic education.

Today, if there is an overall focus on the purpose for education it seems to be on technology. In secondary education, it seems to be on academic preparation for higher education for the top fifty percent of students, but *no one is sure*. Students in the lower fifty percent are tolerated. There is no serious plan to help these students learn a success route within their demonstrated interests or abilities.

Perhaps we should try to peek five to ten years into the future and suggest that we should begin focusing, now, on education's original purpose described by Plato: *To find the goodness within ourselves*. Our society is no longer incensed or disturbed by a growing preponderance of unethical and immoral behavior by our leaders, or common people. Education elitists and policy makers have barred discussions about fair play, respect, courtesy, forgiveness, honor, and morality from classrooms. This leaves no common standard from which our young people might compare themselves for the purpose of maintaining an orderly, kind, tolerant, and progressive society.

Today, that homogeneous society considered important in the early 1900s is no longer considered important by policy makers and others who exercise societal influence. Each separate function having authority transforms into a self-protective tribe, described by Bertrand Russell, that considers only its own selfish ambitions. Each different cultural and ethnic group or identity struggles to maintain its own sub-culture, language, and customs instead of striving toward common interests of an enlightened society. Any attempts to merge common interests and insights to solidify our national priorities and security needs are often rejected with charges of insensitivity, racism, or intolerance. How long can our great nation last with this lack of homogeneity?

Today, do we not tend to blame society - not individuals - for behavior that would not have been tolerated twenty years ago? Can we tell our children they should always be honest and then show them examples where our society respects and supports those who are honest and truthful?

Since society has not defined the purpose, we don't know if the education system is working or not working. If the purpose is to create more jobs for educators, administrators, evaluators, consultants, and critics, then it's certainly working.

Society, including education leaders, political leaders, and other adults, doesn't understand, or cannot clearly and specifically define, the purpose for public education. In any event, they have not clearly announced a defined purpose. Therefore, how should society expect children to understand why they should be marched into a rigidly controlled environment that removes freedom and happiness, eight hours a day, nine months a year, for twelve years of their young lives?

Personal motivation must be preceded by an understood purpose. Many students, although they understand the meaning of the words, are not touched by the feelings of the purpose.

The second major weakness of our education system is that education is discussed and analyzed under one concept, or one umbrella, simply identified as education. There are three parts of education and they must be separated to be properly evaluated and considered. They are: **opportunity, conditions** and **motivation**. Education emphasis focuses almost totally on opportunity, while giving only little regard toward conditions and absolutely none to motivation.

Why is opportunity the only part of education that gets attention from leaders? Could it be that the level and quality of opportunity is determined by the amount of money allocated to that part? Is it possible that money is the only visible effort leaders can show they are 'supporting and improving' education? Is it that this is nothing more than political activity?

The third major weakness is that the education process is based on teaching techniques and teaching theories that focus more on control than on educating. That focus is on teaching, not learning. These techniques and theories suggest students know they must be educated, and they are prepared to receive that education because they have life cycle times of being 'ready to learn' at certain levels.

Even the most enlightened teaching techniques cannot influence students who are de-motivated and drop out of school each year. This includes about thirty percent; with a current accumulation of about four million children between the ages of five and seventeen.

Do political and education leaders consider specific and detailed classroom control more important than results? That's possible; for they continue to micro manage classroom policies and activities. In the meantime, thirty percent of our students drop out of the education process, and teachers become more frustrated because they are not allowed to use their individual talents and personalities in their classrooms to help their students.

Perhaps a homogeneous, prosperous, kind, and tolerant society might not develop to its highest potential in our country until every person is helped and allowed to be successful. Perhaps that success route is individual and personal, and not necessarily the one designed and dictated by education elitists.

Ironically, we must not abandon the possibility that only those students who escape from the standard public education system might be the only students who find success in the original and traditional purpose for education as proposed by Thomas Jefferson: to protect ourselves against tyranny.

Today, many believe our education system has been kidnaped by federal policies determined to move our country from capitalism to *worldism* or socialism. When students are led by teachers to sing praises to a single leader, and not to our country, can the question of a despotic education agenda be discounted? Perhaps the concepts and ideology of 'outcome based education' should also be more closely examined.

Chapter 1

WHAT CREATES LEARNING?

Many things determine how and why one learns. Learning is influenced and determined by leadership, culture, motivations, aspirations, opportunity, conditions, and basic intelligence. These concepts may be identified and explained, but most cannot be used directly in the learning process. These concepts are ordinarily used to explain and rationalize failure in the education process, not to show how to improve that process.

Intelligence is the built-in learning tool. It exists naturally; but must be activated and used to be effective. Three requirements in the learning process are necessary to create that efficiency. These are opportunity, conditions and motivations. These must be understood and addressed individually to maximize our education efforts and resources.

Opportunity allows everyone to participate in the learning process. Most students have opportunity. **Conditions** allow anyone to prepare to participate. Many students and parents are not aware of this preparatory condition. **Motivations** are determined by each student's determination to participate. Despair and fear of the unknown often replace motivations. The following graphic demonstrates that each part is necessary for real education.

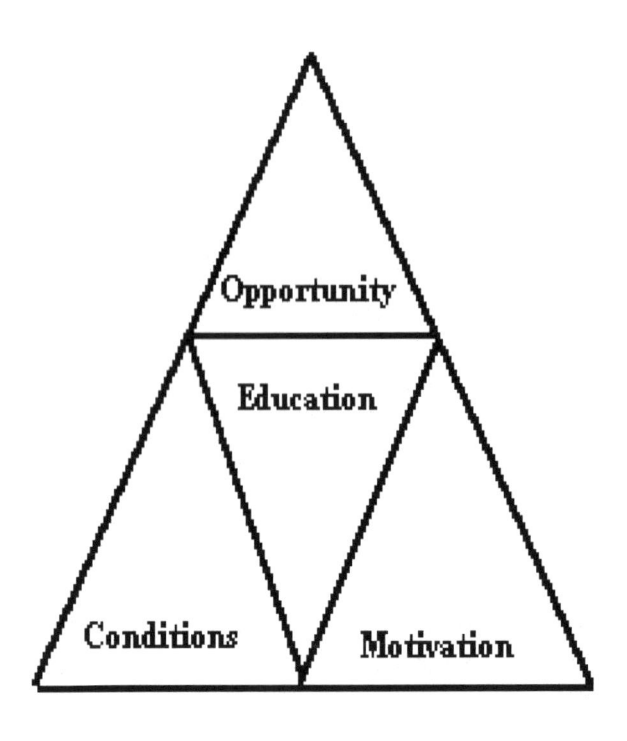

```
           Opportunity
          ────────────
           Education
         /           \
   Conditions    Motivation
```

Opportunity

The opportunity to participate in the learning process is dictated and controlled by governmental agencies and society. They determine where schools will be located, how many schools will exist, what courses will be taught, how many teachers will be hired, the quality of those teachers, the time to spend in class, minimum grades that are acceptable, and disciplinary measures for problem students. These examples demonstrate opportunity. Opportunity refers to the delivery of education to students. All preparations, planning, and decisions regarding education budgets are aimed at this part.

Education budgets are discussed, analyzed and approved regarding only education opportunity. Leaders consider how many classrooms are necessary - and there are never enough to do whatever it is education should do, although that question has never been answered. Teachers' salaries must be budgeted, although there is never enough money to hire enough teachers - to do whatever it is that education should do, or to pay them what they think their work is worth.

Some teachers' groups often imply their work would be better if teachers' pay is better; however, this concept has never proved itself. Ordinarily, higher pay does not produce higher results. In management studies, only profit sharing programs have shown to have any improvement on workplace performance. Higher pay has no effect, except to remove the argument of unfairness for those who think they get less than others for the same work.

Now, in many school communities, education opportunity includes preparing and serving free breakfast to students from low-income families. Although this is a noble concept, and the "moral" thing to do, does it not sever those children from the emotional and physical conditioning they must derive from their parents - *the only source from which it can come?*

Can a child be success-conditioned if the child goes to school realizing his or her parents don't even care enough to prepare the basic subsistence of life, while offering daily guidance over the breakfast table? Worse yet, how many parents stay in bed and never see their children off to school because they don't have to prepare breakfast?

Simply, the more opportunity society tries to deliver to students the more life-skills conditioning they strip from its primary source; the family. Once stripped of most life-skills teaching influence, then society suggests parents should be held more financially accountable for the criminal activities of their children.

Why does the school system, the establishment, keep trying to deliver more opportunity? Is it for humanitarian reasons or from the basic good natures of the individuals in charge? Does the fact they receive more money for more programs have something to do with it? It's unlikely, in education as in any other public endeavor, that the 'good' motive will be a stronger influence than the 'money and power' motive.

Since I live in Mississippi, I will use an event that occurred in that state as an example of the money and power influence over the 'pure education' logic influence.

***

In 1992, the state asked voters to approve a sales tax increase of one percent. Voters were promised the increase would be used for education, since our schools needed so many things to make education more effective, including school supplies, textbooks, smaller classes and a teacher pay raise. Since education is such an emotional topic in Mississippi, as well as the rest of the

Reading Opens Learning Doors

nation, Mississippians overwhelmingly approved the tax increase.

Ordinarily, a reasonable and responsible person would agree we need these fundamental things to help our children become prepared to meet life's challenges, especially textbooks. However, during the time between the passing of the tax increase and the new budgets, all the hoopla and promises were forgotten. Mississippi had saved its education system by passing a tax increase!

What happened? Mississippi still has the same, if not worse, education problems. Mississippi still has the same high dropout rate, the same high illiteracy rate, and the highest teenage birth rate of any state. Nothing has improved in the State's education system except bigger promises that it will get better when more money is available.

Most likely, other schools did the same as the district in which I lived at that time. Instead of budgeting and planning for textbooks, long-range; and instead of hiring teachers to make smaller classes, the district hired more teachers to increase the number of Carnegie units at each school. Instead of making basic education 'better' which was the promise, they made education 'broader' which required even more teachers, without decreasing classroom size.

Ordinarily, the district indoctrinated approximately twelve to fifteen new teachers at the start of each school year. The year after the tax increase, the district indoctrinated more than fifty new teachers, and most of those were for new classes to increase the number of Carnegie units.

A supporter of this idea might suggest this action created 'more opportunity.' A critic might suggest this action ignored basic education fundamentals and created more bragging rights of the district by offering more Carnegie units.

***

This example, although actual, is not necessarily to

criticize the specific decisions and actions in this case. It is merely to demonstrate that education will never be improved until we understand, and make clear to everyone with giant billboards across the nation, the purpose for our education system.

Is it to help every student achieve a working level of literacy, complete with basic life-coping skills; or, is it to offer the highest level of opportunity for those most prepared to accept it? If for the latter case, what happens to those who are not prepared to accept that higher opportunity?

Conditioning

Education conditioning is influenced by things that create life expectations of a child. This ordinarily involves home, cultural and school environments.

A child from a loving, successful, supporting and caring environment will be better conditioned to expect success than will a child from a weaker environment. The successful environment makes it easier for a child to anticipate positive rewards from efforts to make good grades. Many children from weaker cultural environments cannot feel this efforts-results relationship.

Conditions are created and influenced less by words than by feelings and demonstrations. Ordinarily, a child who watches his or her parents struggling to survive, or living in despair because they have given up, is likely to absorb that perspective.

Of course there are exceptions, but normally children who watch their parents and relatives survive in poverty will adopt those survival skills and that economic and social outlook. If it's good enough for parents, why isn't it good enough for the child?

What conditions should a child expect, to allow, and encourage a success attitude? Let's consider those that must exist in two environments.

In schools:

School systems that understand their purpose
Political views that universally support education
Stability in educational leadership
Student priority rather than system priority
Professional and caring teachers
Elimination of distractions - good discipline
Respect among peer students
A comfortable and pleasing environment

In The Home:

Protective and supportive parents
Parents who set good examples for children
Parents who provide basic physiological needs
Parents who care about their child's feelings
Parents who take time to listen to their child
Parents who display self-respect
Parents who respect and care for each other
Parents who treat children as people
Children who are disciplined and courteous
Siblings who support each other
An environment that provides comfort

These are the fundamentals that must exist in school and at home to allow a child to anticipate success. These fundamentals would not necessarily create or enhance student motivation, but they would certainly create a basic environment in which students could find their own internal motivation without negative distractions to deter that motivation.

Motivationist Frederick Herzberg would likely describe these conditions as hygiene factors in his *Motivator-Hygiene Theory*. These are things that do not *create* motivation, within, but *allow* a condition where one might develop motivation to reach certain goals; in this case to develop esteem through success in education.

Motivation

Personal motivation allows any student to gain from the education system regardless of its quality, conditions, or any other influences that affect learning. To learn, a student must plan to learn and take actions that will create that result. That personal motivation usually results from a drive to fulfill a *current* need.

Ordinarily, an uninspired student feels no urgent need to learn - make good grades - because the reward from that effort is not anticipated at the end of the effort. The perceived purpose for education, to prepare for a job to earn money, is too far away to be influencing at the moment. Students are likely to be motivated by different and more current needs.

Those current needs are to feel loved, to feel they belong to a reference group, and to feel important. Students from homes that do not offer positive reinforcement to those needs have no motivating reason to focus their interest on educational success. They struggle to fulfill those basic needs, which they know they will never achieve through good grades, because they are from families that have no history of making good grades. They seek sources outside the education system to fulfill those needs. Often, those sources are undesirable reference groups that provide more immediate esteem.

Those are the same needs that motivate inspired students to make good grades. Successful students are motivated by conditions that anticipate success. They fulfill those needs when they are successful, and gain more positive reinforcement with each need fulfillment. A student's *current need* is not to get a job to provide financial security, for that's the responsibility of the parent or some unseen part of society.

According to motivationists, especially Abraham Maslow and Frederick Herzberg, belonging and esteem are two important motivators once basic physiological needs have been fulfilled. People want to be recognized as part of humanity, and they want to be recognized as a special part of humanity. They seek to feel important; they want to feel important; they *need* to feel important. If they fail to reach goals to fulfill that essential need, many can't feel they are part of normal humanity, and they tend to feel they will never be important.

People, including students, who believe they will never reach a level of importance to satisfy their needs usually suffer from despair and frustration. This despair and frustration continues the negative circle of failure to reach a desired level of importance, or perceived importance. The result is often defensive reactions to those frustrations.

These natural defensive reactions are explained, in-depth, in any basic psychology book. Teachers deal with those negative reactions daily. They include:

Regression: childlike behavior

Some children refuse to accept the responsibility level of their age because they feel they will not gain the rewards of that responsibility. It's more logical for them to pretend not to be serious than to accept the consequences of a failed serious attempt to be successful. Perhaps one who resorts to regression feels he or she will be more acceptable to peers as a fun person than as a more responsible person who fails. Often, an adolescent's actions are more strongly influenced by peer acceptance than by logic.

This condition is not limited to children and adolescents. It can be seen in many frustrated adults who consider themselves beyond that influence of peer pressure. But in our society of trying to appear 'normal' many adults often result to childlike attitudes and actions to hide their frustrations.

Withdrawal: refusing to participate

How often do we hear a frustrated child say, "I can't do that; it's too hard," then watch as the child refuses any further effort to do something? Learning usually requires concentration not only to the task at hand but also to allow the mind to explore to find the controlling concept of the task. Both concentrations must function together for normal learning, and for that learning to have lasting meaning.

The thoughts of many children from low-cultured, low-achievement, or otherwise dysfunctional families often lack the freedom for that level of concentration. Their thoughts, conscious or subconscious, often are absorbed with embarrassment, fear, and more reasons for failure, and that driving desire to feel **important.**

Some withdraw from peer group participation because they simply feel unworthy and unwanted. For them, it's more logical to accept isolation than to risk ridicule. Any child can suffer from this feeling, for it's not necessarily a cultural condition. Often, it's just an individual child's personality.

Aggression: animosity, or refusing to cooperate

Some students are filled with an antisocial personality and rebel against everyone, especially teachers or any other person in an authority position. These students are a teacher's worst nightmare, and often stay just on the brink of actions that would eliminate them from the classroom or the school. They refuse to accept instruction and insist they have a good reason for not doing what they are instructed. For them, the teacher becomes the obstacle and the enemy to their freedom and happiness.

Perhaps students with this condition suffer from either of two influences. First, is the family that shares no loving and understanding feelings within itself. Everyone within the family must participate in a selfish contest to gain an advantage over the others, including the parents.

Secondly, perhaps the child is ignored and given no effective parenting guidance. The child feels independent and resents any interference with his or her decision-making. The child must be in control and must combat anything that would compromise that independence.

Projection: blaming someone else for failing

The defensive mechanism of projection causes one to assume another's feelings or thoughts as justification for failure to overcome an obstacle. In this case, the student doesn't accept the responsibility for the results of his or her efforts. Frequent examples include:

"The teacher hates me! That's why I failed."
"My parents hate me! How can I feel normal?"
"Nobody likes me. Why should I try?"
"Nobody will help me study, so I can learn."
"Who can learn anything at this dumb school?"

Substitution: focusing on a fulfilling endeavor

Students who don't make good grades often make their grades worse by focusing on another activity from which they gain at least some recognition and respect. For example, some boys are skateboard experts because they gain a feeling of importance from that expertise. It's a feeling of importance some know they can't get from grades.

This activity might seem irrational, but one must remember that motivation is created from the drive to fulfill a current need, not one that's in the future or one that's not the driving force. For many children their current need is to feel loved, recognized, and respected. To prepare for a good economic future has no current motivating influence. Students who make good grades get current recognition and high self-esteem from efforts *at that moment*.

According to B.F. Skinner's *operant conditioning* concept, when a student begins to feel rewarded for doing something positive, that creates reinforcement to the action that created the good feeling. Simply, the student learns that the effort will result in success which will gain pride, a high self-image and a good feeling about himself or herself. The student will be more inclined to repeat the process to fulfill that desired need for pride and esteem. Uninspired students haven't learned that process to feel that reward from grades.

SUMMARY

Much confusion still exists from findings of the *Coleman Report,* in 1966. Coleman's data did not support the idea for the survey, commissioned by the Department of Health, Education and Welfare, which was to prove that black students did not have equal access to quality schools, based on financial support and opportunity. His survey revealed that education opportunity was relatively equal, and that educational inequality was caused more by poverty and cultural influences than by race. He found that black students from positive and inspired home environments achieved success as often as white students from the same home environments. Students from both races, reared in poverty and low-cultured environments, had a higher potential to fail or drop out. His controversial conclusion was that it was the supportive culture, not race, that determined educational success for either student.

Instead of recommending racial integration of schools, he suggested social integration, regardless of race. He concluded that a school with no more than forty-percent disadvantaged students mixed with not less than sixty-percent of students from strong education conditions would be a positive peer influence to help the weaker forty-percent. He described this mixing as a form of "social capital," a resource that springs from relations among people, as within successful families.

This situation is the basis for the education confusion of today. It's the foundation of questions regarding busing, magnet schools, and school vouchers. It also explains why disruptive and uninspired students are given such wide latitude to remain in and disrupt today's classrooms.

Coleman was immediately labeled a racist by many of his

peers who supported the race-only idea. Even the president of the American Sociological Association tried to have him expelled from that organization for his findings, although those conclusions were based on studies of 600,000 students at 4000 schools. Later he was exonerated and became president of that organization.

Chapter 2

OUR WORST EDUCATION PROBLEM

Traditionally, individual education effectiveness has been judged by grades, and over-all in a community by the success of students performing in the real world after they leave school. The current trend is to judge education effectiveness by comparing scores on national measurement tests.

The underlying assumption is that a school with higher scores on those comparative tests will have better opportunity, and therefore will produce more successful students. Otherwise, what is the reason or practicality for those measurements?

Proponents of those tests proclaim the results reveal areas of weakness in schools or school districts that must be improved. Supposedly, the purpose of this testing is to create more or better opportunity for students to learn. This justification lacks a sound or practical basis. This rationality merely assumes the purpose for education is to produce high grades in those subjectively selected areas of measurement. Until society announces a clear and positive definition for the purpose for education what relationship do the results of those subjective tests have with educational success? That definition does not exist, therefore what is the benchmark for the measurements?

For example, if our national education policy is to insure every student leaves school with the ability to read at least at an eighth-grade level, certainly any local teacher would know if a student can read at that level. It doesn't take a national test to confirm that status. If our national education policy is to insure each graduate has basic job skills, a national test could not confirm that status. Job centers or businesses could confirm that status by being anxious to hire more of those graduates as their workers.

Our focus is totally on improving student grades - *in those areas that are measured.* This is a measurement of education opportunity, schools, and teachers; not aspirations, motivation and real student achievement. Is that focus to make successful students more successful? Does education elitism suggest that students who make higher A's will be more successful than students who make lower A's? If school curricula are geared to making higher scores on those tests, is our education system more concerned about the image of the system and bragging rights,or the success of individual students and the contribution they might make to our society? Should we not encourage and assist all students and other young people to learn how to *get to the end of the row*, rather than running from the snakes and giving up in despair?

Society and many education elitists undoubtedly ignore the possibility that one student's C is an achievement greater than another student's A. The student who makes that C should be offered the same love and respect as the student who makes the A. That is, of course, until and unless we establish our education objective that every student must make those A grades. When that happens, perhaps education elitists and politicians might also add that students who make grades other than A should be banished to an unnamed island so they may be ignored and forgotten.

We all are not endowed with identical academic potential, or comprehensibility. We are different, with different talents and capabilities. Many C students succeed in real life far greater than

A students. Even a D or F student who isn't stripped of hope and aspirations often makes great contributions to our society.

We should not strip the C student from his or her earned respect. If a C is a passing grade, it should be regarded as a passing grade. After all, children do not volunteer to come into our world to be compared with other students who have higher natural abilities. They want to be loved and respected, as does any other human want to be loved and respected.

Regarding those national tests: schools proclaim to teach at their full capacity, now. What will be given up or sacrificed to focus on those areas in which tests reveal weaknesses? Do we eliminate Civics, Geography, Health and Arts from classrooms? Does our education system have that capacity?

So, what is the most important statistic regarding education effectiveness? Considering education from all perspectives the greatest statistic that affects individuals, and society, is the dropout rate. Students who stay in school and do the best they can still have hope and aspirations for the future. Their success potential is unlimited. Those who give up and drop out defeat themselves and are the most likely to contribute to other important social statistics: crime and poverty.

A high dropout rate in a low-achieving district reflects the conditions and demographic composition of the community, and produces serious results for society. The graphic on the next page shows this dropout-poverty-crime relationship.

Education-Demographic Relationships

State	%White	Grad. Rate	Poverty Rate	Burglary Robbery
				Per 100,000

Lowest Graduation Rates - Ten States

	1995	2005	1994	2004	1996	2006	1996	2006
SC	69	68	55.1	60.6	16.5	13.1	1556	1126
GA	71	66	56.6	61.2	13.5	13.5	1319	1074
LA	67	64	58.7	69.4	20.1	17.6	1572	1182
FL	83	80	59.1	66.4	15.2	11.3	1810	1142
TX	75	83	59.7	76.7	17.0	16.3	1239	1115
MS	64	61	60.1	62.7	22.1	20.4	1266	1043
D.C.	30	38	60.1	68.2	23.2	19.8	2996	1317
AL	74	71	60.2	65.0	17.1	15.5	1168	1122
NY	74	74	61.8	60.9	16.6	14.3	1051	523
AZ	81	87	63.2	66.8	18.3	14.8	1423	1075
AVG	68.8	69.2	59.5	65.7	18	15.7	1540	1072

Highest Graduation Rates - Ten States

	1995	2005	1994	2004	1996	2006	1996	2006
VT	99	97	89.4	85.4	11.5	7.7	688	546
ND	95	92	86.8	86.0	11.5	11.3	320	387
MN	94	89	86.8	84.7	9.5	8.1	877	689
SD	92	88	86.6	83.7	13.2	11.3	576	387
MT	93	91	85.6	80.4	16.2	13.7	587	328
IA	97	95	85.1	85.8	10.9	10.8	710	646
NE	94	92	84.3	87.6	9.9	9.9	680	598
NJ	79	76	83.5	86.3	8.5	7.8	1028	605
WI	92	90	81.7	85.8	8.7	10.2	684	586
ID	94	95	79.5	81.5	13.2	9.7	729	533
AVG	92.9	90.5	85	84.7	11.3	10.0	623	530

Estimates extracted from The World Almanac and Book of Facts:1998-2008
Average of totals are not by population but for reference comparison only.

Chapter 3

CREATING EFFECTIVE EDUCATION

Our education dropout rate is a far more serious problem than grades. Simply, a student who stays in school and graduates does not eliminate himself or herself from the normal possibility of success. At minimum, a student who does not drop out does not isolate himself or herself from the norms and expectations as citizens of our society.

The data also strongly suggest a child from a background of failure and despair is likely to adopt that pattern even when the best conditions exist in the school environment. The child's failure is from the home and cultural environment, not from any weakness in a normal and caring society.

At this time, before we discuss how to improve education effectiveness for everyone, we should consider an alternative position. We should consider the position that not everyone in America can - and should - be educated. This might be considered a preposterous concept, but it's also a concept that should not totally be discounted. Consider the new ideas of 'outcome based education' and 'global citizenship.'

Some in our society believe that if everyone becomes too educated we will not have a pool of workers from which to hire for menial and laborious jobs. Do we need a large group of people who are worthy of only minimum wage jobs? Some in our society suggest this necessity. We have the ability to train everyone who is capable of being successful. Why haven't we done it?

If we really are sincere about education effectiveness, and want to make it the best it can be, then we should do something to demonstrate our concern. We should not *just talk* and keep it at the political issue level. Perhaps the six National Education Goals 2000 is the perfect example of all talk, political rhetoric, and no action. We were presented with grandiose goals for education, but they were goals with no substance or purpose. Consequently, they were doomed to fail from inception. It's unlikely that even one percent of our population even knows one of the six goals. Briefly, they are: By the year 2000:

1. **All children in America will start school ready to learn.**

2. **The high school graduation rate will increase to at least 90 percent.**

3. **American students will leave grades 4, 8, and 12 having demonstrated competency in challenging subject matter.**

4. **U.S. students will be first in the world in science and mathematics achievement.**

5. **Every adult American will be literate and will possess the knowledge and skills necessary to compete in a global economy, and exercise the right and responsibilities of citizenship.**

6. **Every school in America will be free of drugs and violence, and will offer a disciplined environment conducive to learning.**

Although these are high and noble goals, they lack two basic essentials. First, they do not describe the purpose for education. Secondly, they give no alternatives for people who can't achieve them. Nevertheless, these goals were intended to guide our education efforts. The year 2000 has long since passed and nothing in that plan has been accomplished except to create more incentive for more students to drop out of school. A school's targeted scores become higher if fewer of the weaker students are left to take those required tests.

The latest grandiose scheme is the "No Child Left Behind" program. It has no greater probability of success than did the Goals 2000 plan, and for the same reasons. The focus is on cloning students, not offering each child an opportunity to be motivated through realistic and personal aspirations.

A New Approach

An education system we perceive as being effective must have a foundation or benchmark from which to judge or determine that effectiveness. Then, anything that results in success must be accomplished through motivation. Motivation must be based on a clear goal, a perceived need to reach that goal, and confidence that the expended energy and effort will result in achieving that goal.

That motivation must be for the targets of education: students - not the producers of education: the system.

Currently, students who function within education norms do so based on three motivation principles. The top students find high prestige, a self-fulfillment factor based on their expectations of themselves.

The second level, those who do well but not the best, desire to belong to the normal group. Their belonging needs are fulfilled by 'passing.' They feel normal by considering themselves not to be a bookworm, above their peer group.

Those who barely pass do so for security needs, one of the basic primitive needs. They fear the unknown of failure. That fear often is reinforced by threats from parents.

That leaves the twenty-five to thirty percent who eventually fail or drop out. Certainly, many of these students lack the mental skills to compete in an education environment that is hell-bent on raising graduation standards to demonstrate the education system is effective. Most, however, have the ability but lack the cultural conditioning to compete. Our fundamental education question is: **Do we want to educate these children - or continue to toss them aside from a system that doesn't consider their needs?**

The Foundation

The foundation of personal motivation must be a goal. And, that goal must be perceived as real and attainable by those asked to participate. Students are the objects of education and they are asked to participate. Many do not understand the goal or have the feeling they are capable of achieving it. The goal doesn't seem applicable to some.

Possible alternative goals were earlier identified, but none was identified as being regarded as a fixed target. Since we are an economic based society, it's not unreasonable to conclude that the basic target, the goal, of education should be:

To prepare for independence and happiness.

This goal targets the job and it also allows individuals to consider higher personal goals along the process. Those who need to feel more important are allowed that option; those who need to feel they belong also are allowed that option. Those who simply seek security are aiming at the same target, while at the same time not infringing upon the rights and goals of others.

Most crime is aimed at financial gain and independence, but crime is not acceptable to a normal society, nor does it create happiness. Welfare support is a form of independence, but it also infringes upon the rights of those who must sacrifice part of their effort to achieve their goals, in the form of higher taxes. It doesn't ordinarily create or support happiness by the recipient. It has no basis for one to have a feeling of accomplishment.

Ordinarily, tax is the payment of a fair share to be part of something positive. However, when that fair share does not benefit the contributor, in any way, then it's an abusive penalty for all persons. The person who must pay more taxes to give money and support to others is penalized for succeeding. The person who receives that support, for no effort, is eliminated from a feeling of belonging, importance, and self worth, an expectation of normal humanity and happiness.

The goal must be simple enough for anyone to understand in depth sufficiently to encourage motivation. This is particularly true for children, since they are so easily distracted and refocused with new stimuli that change every moment, especially the stimuli that affect their feelings. Children understand the meaning of the word "happiness." Happiness involves current feelings and influences under which they respond. For young children, the word "happiness" includes the concepts of love, belonging and caring. These are the current needs upon which they focus their current motivation.

They must also understand that a job, which creates and allows independence, is necessary for them to reach that level of happiness they desire. A job, for reasons of security, is not a currently felt need for most American children; for is that not the purpose for parents. Providing parents who exist are current, not some absence foreseen in the future.

The Education Process

A process, as in the 'Education System,' must begin with a fundamental premise. An illiterate person once made a statement that establishes this premise. That statement was, *"An illiterate person does not even know how to be friendly."*

This statement was made by a young woman attending the statewide Literary Conference in Jackson, Mississippi, in 1995, where I had the honor of being the keynote speaker. Her goal was to learn how to read so she could join what she considered 'normal' society. If we accept this purpose for education, and if we accept this premise, then we must focus early education on **reading**.

Every child in school must know how to read within acceptable levels before any other topic or subject becomes relevant. Does it matter if a child knows that London is in England, if the child can't read well enough to recognize 'London' on a map? Does it matter that a child can do algebraic equations if the child can't read well enough to understand that an algebraic equation applies? In our society, does it matter that a person can read signs that dictate: Stop, Caution, Proceed at you own risk, Yield to pedestrians, Children at play, One-way street or Danger ahead?

Can a person find happiness, or a fulfilled life, if that person can't read? Can a person find happiness if that person doesn't know *how to be friendly?* Can that person positively contribute to a healthy society? Not likely.

If we accept this goal of education, then reading must take precedence over all other academic teaching. Simply, a child who can't read can't learn from things written. *A child who can't learn can never be happy.*

Furthermore, the concept of reading should be expanded to

include speed reading. Some students read, but read so slowly the meaning is often not comprehended, or lost, because reading of individual words is so slow. Comprehension must be supported by thoughts and ideas presented by groups of words and sentences, not just individual words. I did not understand this concept until I was in Air Force basic training where speed reading was one of the training programs. Reading speed and comprehension can easily be tripled or quadrupled, which enhances the learning process.

The second most important target must be **mathematics.** Our society functions from numbers, as well as from written words. But, must those numbers include complex algebraic equations for students who will never have any use for them, other than to satisfy the ego needs of a test designer? Is it possible the requirement for advanced algebra and science in secondary schools is dictated more by the ego of the education system and an embarrassed society trying to justify itself than by the needs of the average student?

The proof of this question is self-evident, at this very moment. Do you, as the reader, understand the definition of a compound fractional equation? Can you now solve one? Do you know the definition, use or order arrangement of the Pythagorean theorem? Have you survived well, and happily, without knowing these things? If you are reading this book, without difficulty, then of course you have.

I was reintroduced to these terms while teaching a GED student, and as a substitute teacher at a local middle school. Even while I taught these concepts, I knew they would never be used by those students. I knew the time could be used more effectively by teaching something more practical and useful, such as reading and writing.

So why must our young students spend hours of frustration focusing on these tasks, which are meaningless and useless for most people, except those planning for a degree that requires advanced mathematics. Most students would gain much more, educationally and practically, by improving their reading, basic mathematics, and social and human relations skills.

Often, these higher-level and complex tasks confirm what a low-self-esteemed young student already knows: that they must be unworthy, because the 'normal world with better people' is too complex for them. And, if they are unworthy, why try to compete? It's easier and eliminates their frustration and embarrassment if they drop out of school. It's those current needs that motivate people to action not those needs, seen or unseen, in the future.

Would an average person, child or adult, want to remain in an environment that created only embarrassment, frustration, and failure? Most would say, "NO!"

But, alas, society and our leaders in the education system complain that too many children don't take advantage of such wonderful education opportunities in our country. "Those children just don't understand."

After The Basics

When should the concentrated focus on reading and fundamental mathematics end? When the child demonstrates proficiency at the level required by society. That is, to the level of understanding things written by society, which would include, at minimum: books, newspapers, posted signs, public information brochures and official instructions.

Most people understand the requirement for normal use of numbers. That requirement does not include advanced algebra. Surveys often reveal that some students who learn algebra don't even know how to balance their checkbooks.

The next educational focus should be turned toward the success target of the student, not the success or failure alternative of the student. Consider an athletic competition event as an example:

Professional football teams compete against other professional teams. College football teams compete against other college football teams. High school football teams compete against other high school football teams. Would a high school football team - any high school football team - expect to compete successfully against a professional football team? Of course not. It's likely that a high school football player might expect to be injured competing against a professional football player. The professional is better prepared and better conditioned.

Using this example, is it unreasonable to imagine that a student who expects to fail might be injured by a student who knows how to succeed? A conditioned and trained student would not intend to injure a non-conditioned student, as a professional athlete would not plan to injure a less mature athlete. But, in the academic environment, it happens. It happens because that's how the education system is organized. It forces weak conditioned students to compete with well conditioned students. Almost a third drop out of the competition, while others remain in an atmosphere of despair and defeat.

In effect, our education system is designed to destroy the aspirations and happiness of many students. But, what can we do that's fair to everyone? They must be educated.

If we accept the suggested purpose for education, then the process is simple. The purpose must dictate and direct the process.

Those who need to learn the basics and fundamentals, to allow them to find a job and happiness, should be taught the basics and fundamentals. Those who are well prepared and conditioned, and more motivated toward higher success goals, should be allowed to reach for those goals. This concept introduces the question of high school diplomas.

Is it unreasonable to consider the idea that high schools should have different types of diplomas recognizing different student goals and objectives? This might be an unusual concept, but colleges and universities have been doing it for centuries.

Why should a student who simply needs and wants to prepare for a job be forced to compete academically with a student who wants and needs a piece of paper, called a diploma, to go to college? A diploma, a record of success at some endeavor, should fill different needs, especially for positive students with different abilities and skills.

With almost a third of our children dropping out of school, and many more barely tolerating it with failing grades, is this even a conscionable concept in a humane society? It's just what we do, because it's what we have always done; because anything different might be too risky and controversial. It might not be politically correct to target education directly at education effectiveness. Perhaps it's politically safer to treat all students as assembly line robots than to accept the idea that some are different with different needs to help them succeed.

An education system based on this concept must consider other conditions which would include diploma identifications such as **Academic** diploma and **Special** or **Skills** diploma? For job purposes, society should consider both as high school diplomas. One holding a Skills diploma should not be denied access to higher education if he or she demonstrates proficiency for entry into that environment. Maturity later changes the attitudes, motivations and study effectiveness of many.

The requirements for a **Special** diploma should be focused more on readiness than on grades. The child should not be allowed to 'fail,' but should remain in the process until he or she reaches the minimum qualifications for a job that requires a high school diploma. The terms 'fail' and 'dropout' must be eliminated from our school dictionary, regardless of the amount of effort required by society to prevent that from happening.

We must not forget that a failing child is the most highly qualified candidate for our prison system, and is more likely to participate in erosion of our civilized society. A failing child might become one of the greatest supporters and contributors to our society if given a chance to do what he or she prefers to do rather than yield to the dictates, expectations, and plans of society.

Our education system must consider young students as individuals; with different attitudes, abilities, needs, and happiness aspirations, rather than as boxes spewing from an assembly line. Products that flow from an assembly line are made from identical components. Each child has unique parts and components, in their brains and environments, that do not facilitate assembly line manipulation and control.

Each child views the world differently, as do adults, and must be allowed to develop his or her fullest potential for success and happiness in the best way that fits each individual. Children who look forward to a future of something - anything positive - are greater assets to America, and to themselves, than is a child who suffers despair and defeat, and drops out.

With despair, however, we must acknowledge that it's unlikely that political and education leaders have the will or the stability to change the education system enough to make it truly effective and responsive to students' needs. They see the risk as simply too great, for they might lose control of a system that's now the source of huge budgets.

One of our modern philosophers, Bertrand Russell, perhaps described our education dilemma best:

"It is because modern education is so seldom inspired by a great hope that it so seldom achieves a great result. The wish to preserve the past rather than the hope of creating the future dominates the minds of those who control the teaching of the young."

Regardless, those who care enough to task ourselves with expressions of hope for a better society, along with the risks of criticism and disdain that often accompany those expressions, must continue along that process as best we can. Writers and critics must continue to identify those things that might be and could be, to keep hope alive.

The status quo of established systems is protected by a powerful and vicious defense. Also, according to Bertrand Russell in his book, *Authority and the Individual*, the survival and perpetuation of a group formed for a noble and good purpose often becomes more important than the purpose for which the group was established. The group becomes a *tribe* which must continue to exist regardless of its effectiveness or the resulting consequences.

Dedicated teachers bear the greatest burden of all. Even as they get little support from society, they continue to keep hope alive by demonstrating positive success attitudes to children whose eager eyes anticipate their readiness to help, and their exemplary leadership, day after day after day.

Concerned parents also have little or no influence in

designing or changing the system charged with educating their children. Parents who register complaints are most often ridiculed by the 'system' as trouble-makers who don't understand education. Ordinarily, the complaint is registered, the complainant is criticized, then the question is dropped. It's the familiar tactic of the best defense is a strong offense.

Nevertheless, regardless of the quality of our education system, there is always hope of education success for any child. Even in our current education system we have many successful students and many wonderful success stories. Research and surveys reveal, however, that most students' education success is determined by the concern, examples and leadership of the parents and by the attitude of the student.

Reading Opens Learning Doors

Chapter 4

A SUCCESS PLAN

Regardless of our ability or inability to determine the fundamental purpose for education, the education process must become more effective if we expect to sustain a progressive and nurturing society that will allow personal and individual success. Although the education process might be made more efficient if all known variables were considered, that doesn't suggest the process cannot be improved. Even with the limitations of lack of education focus, a non-supportive society, uninspired educators, and cultural weaknesses, education effectiveness can be improved. The current education establishment, however, must take a more universal perspective to make that possible.

A new perspective requires educators and society to focus more on developing a more confident and adaptable student rather than on developing a specifically educated student. Government and educators in the secondary education system seem focused only on higher education; college. That's a limited focus and a distraction to what might be the grandest purpose education might achieve: improvement of society and the individual. These goals are certainly important, and essential, but we must not forget two other important needs of education. One is that which was a major concern of Thomas Jefferson: *that we be educated to prevent political tyranny.* The other is Plato's description of the purpose for education: *to find the goodness within ourselves.*

Now, education is focused on competitive grades to sort out, *to eliminate*, those considered below standard. If this is not true, then why are tests graded on a curve designed to fail some students, or to label them in the bottom ten percent or twenty percent? To develop a more progressive and responsive society, should education's focus not be to include and prepare more citizens for a broader contributing and more responsible society?

Simply, the education system and society must not allow any student to fail, or to consider himself or herself a failure. All students must be prepared for something, and they must be allowed to feel that accomplishment. Students who don't have the ability to be a rocket scientist or a brain surgeon should not be measured and evaluated against those who do have that ability.

To be successful, students must be prepared to anticipate changes, transitions, and new challenges they will face in the future. Education emphasis must be focused toward four specific areas to accomplish that goal. Those four areas include: **how to learn, communications and comprehension, success planning, and general workplace skills.**

While we analyze these four concepts we must remember they apply primarily to students who don't know how to use their innate abilities. High achieving students will likely continue to be high achieving students regardless of this emphasis, for there continues to be many high achieving students in any education environment, even in failing schools. They succeed, and most likely will continue, even in our education environment that doesn't understand its purpose.

According to the Pareto Principle, approximately twenty percent of our students will be high achievers regardless of the conditions in which they must learn. The purposes for these new approaches are to increase the number of high achieving students and to give new optimism to other students so they might free themselves from their feelings of self doubt and inferiority. According to the Pareto Principle this includes approximately the lowest twenty to twenty-five percent of students. These four approaches to accomplish these goals will be analyzed next.

Learning How to Learn

Learning how to learn is a subject ignored in most schools. Our current education system seems to use the approach that if information is fed into empty shells (brains) and then reinforced by feedback through the evaluation and testing process, learning automatically will occur. Obviously, this assumption has been used for generations though it's not proven to be valid.

This assumption, or lack of a more effective assumption, has allowed the teaching and learning process to remain less effective. More simply stated: if we want students to learn something that's worth learning then we should teach them how to learn. Now, we don't. Our education system has ignored this important first step in the learning process.

An example that demonstrates the importance of learning to learn in the education process is the concept of learning to teach in the education process. Teachers are not only taught their subject specialties such as mathematics, science and economics, they also are taught how to teach. They are given the basic information and they are taught how to convey that basic information during the education process.

Students are usually given only the basic information. They are not taught how to receive, to accept, or to assimilate that basic information, or even what to do with it when they understand how to receive it. Weak students don't understand the receiving process or the relevance of the information to real world application. This confirms the conclusion that education does not apply, or even consider, motivation principles.

To resolve this problem, schools must teach a basic study skills course. There are some schools and some classrooms that attempt to do it, however those attempts usually are unorganized.

Study skills are casually encouraged by some teachers, but a study skills program doesn't exist in most public education systems to demonstrate the importance of really knowing how to learn.

Well meaning educators discuss the learning process only as they have time during their busy schedules, or as they happen to think of an important idea to help a desperate student or parent after the damage has occurred. Those specific study skills are detailed in another chapter.

Students must not only be taught how to learn, they must also be taught how to use new knowledge when they learn it. The second basic education need, communications and comprehension, must be taught to help students learn what to do with that new learning. It also helps them learn it better, because they will understand the purpose for that learning. That need will be considered next.

Communications and Comprehension

The ability to communicate effectively is one of the major success determinants. The ability to comprehend and understand related concepts through active cognition is another of the determinants to individual success. Although these two traits are related, since they both involve mental and psychological interactions, they will be discussed separately for clarity and simplicity.

Communications

To learn, to learn how to learn, and to use what one has learned require the effective use of communications. Schools are obviously aware of the importance of the communications process, for they ordinarily conduct courses on the basic elements of communications. These courses usually include the proper use of grammar, basic appreciation of prose and poetry, and a few short speeches in the classroom. Although these standard courses are essential to teach those basic elements, they aren't sufficient to teach the full scope of communications that's essential to help a student become successful.

Schools must also teach students how to use that basic knowledge of communication fundamentals. Students are taught the what of communications, but they ordinarily are not taught the how, which is the application of communications. There's a significant difference in these approaches. The what provides the tool. The how demonstrates how to use the tool. One must practice to learn how to use any tool, even a tool as basic as a hammer.

Some might ask, "Why should schools be tasked to teach students how to communicate once they have been given that fundamental knowledge? Shouldn't they learn that process during their social interactions and in their family environments?" The answers to these questions are self evident when it's recalled that this information doesn't apply to those upper goal directed and naturally successful students. Those naturally gifted and inspired students would succeed despite the weaknesses of any education system.

This progressive approach is intended to help students with less cultural support to learn how to become successful. This includes the lower twenty to twenty-five percent. These students need a different approach to learn effective communications. This is the social capital James Coleman described.

The active use of communications, regardless of the knowledge of the communications process, is influenced more in a child's home and cultural environment than in the artificial education environment. Even if a child in a home of low cultural support takes the knowledge of effective communications into his or her home, that knowledge is not used or reinforced by practice. That use and reinforcement must be learned and practiced in the school environment so thoroughly that the positive environment will have more influence than the more negative environment of the child's primary influencing culture.

Knowing how to use a hammer is not enough to use a hammer effectively. The only way to learn how to use a hammer is to use it until it becomes a natural extension of one's hand. Neither is merely knowing how to communicate enough to be able to communicate.

Once this goal becomes clear, the process to fill that need becomes relatively easy. A course titled *Active Communications* should be established and required for each school year, beginning in the sixth grade. This course could be somewhat flexible in content, but would fulfill at least the following essentials. All students must:

- Participate in casual group conversations
- Participate in formal group assignments
- Learn to lead group discussions
- Learn how to tell jokes and anecdotes
- Learn how to summarize a group discussion
- Learn how to initiate a conversation
- Learn to communicate with different age groups
- Learn how to criticize positively
- Learn how to accept criticism
- Learn how to speak extemporaneously
- Learn how to be poised when speaking
- Learn how to debate and negotiate

The overriding purpose of this course is to allow a student, over a long period of time, to develop inherent confidence in his or her abilities to be part of society, and not merely part of a narrow culture. Image and self esteem are the ultimate goals of this process. With enough self esteem, a student from a lower culture in society is not handicapped by that culture. The student learns in the Active Communications class that he or she is as intelligent and as worthy as all other students, regardless of social or economic status.

Behaviorists Berelson and Steiner defined this cultural handicap as *narrow personality*. This condition must be addressed and corrected to allow the education system to work. Otherwise, effective education will never be achieved for the lower twenty to twenty-five percent of our student population.

Two things are critical to enhance the effectiveness of this class. First, the teacher must be one who earns respect and admiration from students. Second, a grading system should not be relevant to this class. The question should not be, 'Has this student earned an A or an F?' The question should be, 'Can this student communicate well and comfortably in general society?' If a person can't communicate well, what relevance is a grade?

Another consideration would make this class even more meaningful and effective. People in the business community and the retired community should be part of this classroom interaction, not necessarily in the role of teacher or advisor but in the role of a mutual participant. This would help to eliminate the common belief by culturally deprived students that other normal people in business and society are significantly different in basic abilities and intelligence. The fundamental purpose for this class is cultural assimilation into the expected norms of society.

Comprehension

Since comprehension is one of the cognitive skills it cannot be isolated for separate training. Therefore, it should be taught and reinforced in the same Active Communications class. The other important cognitive skills might be identified as assimilation and conceptualization. This analysis will consider only comprehension, for the others might improve from increased comprehension; it's not certain they can be taught.

The purpose for an Active Communications class is to train reluctant students, probably by strong encouragement at first, to understand and emotionally to feel that they have minds and real intelligence that can be activated to function on the same level as anyone else in society. When they are forced into the mini-society of the Active Communications classroom they will not have an opportunity to remain locked within that narrow personality Berelson and Steiner describe. They will be forced by class participation to expand their narrow personality.

When that narrow personality becomes expanded it must be occupied by something. That something should be increased comprehension. Once comprehension is increased within these culturally or emotionally deprived students, they are then able to develop meaningful confidence and self esteem. This becomes the basis for each individual's success.

Confidence and self esteem must be encouraged and reinforced by understanding the success process. That process will be introduced next and is identified as success planning. Success planning should also be taught as part of the normal school curriculum - in a formal classroom. This concept should also be the primary source of topics in the Active Communications class.

Success Planning

Unsuccessful people assume success either happens or it doesn't. That might be the case for some people, but success 'just happens' so infrequently that this accidental event cannot be planned as a basis for a successful future. Ordinarily one must plan to be successful to be successful. Norman Vincent Peale once wrote, 'You can be greater than anything that can happen to you.'

Success planning is based on that concept.

Becoming successful must be a planned event. In the normal process of succeeding, things and actions must be considered and planned. Once they are planned, they must then be done. Success planning includes the following actions:

1. Understanding goals
2. Developing a success attitude
3. Avoiding demotivation
4. Self development
5. Avoiding frustration
6. Improving communications skills
7. Improving interpersonal relationships

These are the simple success planning factors that often are identified as the secrets of success. Since we don't want them to be secrets we must understand how simple they are. These secrets, except 'avoiding demotivation,' briefly will be considered next.

Understanding Goals

Success is determined by accomplishing goals. If one doesn't assign goals then he or she cannot accomplish those goals. Instead of having a plan for success, one will have a definite plan for failure.

A misunderstanding of goals, however, may also cause failure. Students often are advised by parents, teachers or other authority figures to assign goals to themselves, but many aren't able to do that clearly enough to establish a target for success. Understanding goals is important in the process of assigning goals, for one might think he or she has assigned a goal when, in fact, that person has not.

Reading Opens Learning Doors

Goals may be identified by two types and two dimensions. The two clearly identifiable types of goals include short-term goals and long-term goals. This concept of short-term and long-term goals seems simple enough, but many never reach success because they don't understand the implication of the relationship between these two goals.

Short-term goals must be met to fulfill long-term goals. Too often a person assigns himself or herself a long-term goal that's so distant it becomes unreachable. Those long-term goals are reached by assigning and reaching a series of short-term goals. The success process is learned through achieving short-term goals. The long-term goal evolves naturally. This concept could be called *the magic of little wins*.

Successfully achieving long-term goals is determined by reaching a series of short-term goals. If it's that simple, why isn't it easy for everyone to become successful? It is easy, but there's usually one major problem; the fear or the unwillingness to take the first step of the first short-term goal. Most unsuccessful people fail to take that first simple step, or they quit when the first step seems too difficult. They face the cultural blockade. Two common examples involve college.

Many high school graduates plan to get a college degree; however, only a few actually follow through to reach that goal. Actually getting that college degree usually is not determined by desire, by cost, by need, or by intelligence. That success is more often determined when graduates assign a short-term goal of going to the college to enroll. Others only plan to go to the college to enroll - someday.

Another reason some high school graduates don't get their college degree is that they can't wait to get the degree. Each individual course is considered an insurmountable obstacle rather than a short-term goal. Those who fail focus on the long-term dream and not the realistic short-term goals of each individual course.

Although understanding the differences and inferences of short-term goals and long-term goals is important, there are other equally important considerations of goals. These include goal dimensions: definite and indefinite.

Often, someone thinks he or she has assigned himself or herself a goal when, in fact, that hasn't occurred. That person might have assigned an indefinite goal which is really not an attainable goal.

A definite goal is one that may be described, identified and achieved, or reached. It's also one that can be measured along the way.

For example, how many times have you heard someone say, "My goal in life is to save enough money to retire on when I get old, so I can live happily ever after?" This common statement is a primary cause of failure for many people. There's a fundamental flaw with this goal that makes it unreachable. That fundamental flaw is that this isn't really a goal. It cannot be measured, and it cannot be understood if it's reached. Two concepts make this goal unreachable.

First, many people never feel they are old. At what age would this person consider as the right age for that goal? Second, the exact amount of money needed for retirement hasn't been identified. Is it $100,000, $200,000 or two million dollars? Clearly, this common idea is not a goal for it can't be measured along the way or identified when it's achieved.

A definite goal would be, "I plan to save $100,000 and retire when I reach the age of sixty-five." Both conditions are identifiable and can be measured between the beginning and the ending. At age fifty-five, one would know he or she has only ten more years until that planned retirement age. If that person has saved $30,000, then he or she would know the money target is about thirty percent complete. This is a definite goal.

People don't fail to reach goals because they can't reach those goals. They fail to reach goals because:

They only dream of long-term goals
They fail to assign clear short-term goals
They don't assign definite and identifiable goals
They fail to take the most important first step.

People who fail obviously don't understand the importance of assigning and striving to reach simple goals. They tend to over dramatize and over complicate a simple process.

Developing a Success Attitude

Isn't it amazing how some people who dream of being successful are defeated with a negative and grumpy attitude before they begin? Before they even assign themselves a short term goal, if they understand that process, they lament that, "It's probably not going to work, anyway." If they have any possibility of becoming successful, it's only because they accidentally step into it, which is rare. Ordinarily, success happens because it's made to happen.

Developing and displaying a success attitude is one of the most important requirements to become successful. Many people are fortunate enough to have developed a good attitude or a success attitude, naturally. Others, however, have difficulty in this process, for it doesn't occur naturally; even if they desperately want to display a happy, optimistic, and successful attitude.

The following steps will explain to those who want to develop a success attitude how to do it. This process is identified as the DASA (Developing a Success Attitude) plan. The DASA plan includes the following steps:

Start the day okay
Learn to be relaxed

Emulate positive people
Continue self improvement
Learn to empathize
Practice self-evaluation.

Start the day okay

One of the major secrets to success is for a person to feel he or she deserves, or is entitled to, success. A person who has this feeling anticipates good events and conclusions. One who doesn't have this feeling doesn't expect good things to happen. A feeling of anticipating good things to happen allows those good things to happen and doesn't block them.

The same events usually occur to everyone. It's only the reaction and response to those events by each individual that determine that person's success or failure.

To start the day okay is a simple process. One simply determines to begin the day positively instead of negatively or unconcerned. If one starts the day unconcerned, normal negative influences and surroundings may cause that person to develop negative tendencies without realizing what's happened. One may be sure of beginning the day with a positive feeling only by intending to begin the day with a positive feeling about himself or herself. A person begins the day okay simply by telling himself or herself at the beginning of each day that he or she is a good person to whom good things will happen.

Learn to be relaxed

A person cannot maximize his or her abilities and confidence in situations of apprehension and tension. To understand and develop a success attitude, one must develop a self presence that will allow that person to concentrate on solving problems, instead of worrying about their existence. Worrying about problems has never solved any problems. Trying to avoid problems has never solved any problems. Believing that one is not capable of solving problems prevents other problems from being solved.

The correct way to solve problems and questions is to focus on finding solutions, not to worry about their existence. To find solutions one must be prepared to accept problems as natural occurrences and be prepared to handle them. Consequently, the key to being relaxed to handle problems is to be prepared for their occurrence.

One might ask, "How can a football quarterback make decisions so quickly and accurately within split seconds while people are trying to pounce all over him?" One might also ask, "How can a matador in the bull ring remain so calm while a mad bull is trying to gore him with two giant horns." Another equally interesting question is, "How can a ballerina dance on her toes for an hour and make those motions seem effortless?"

These questions have a simple answer: they planned, practiced, and prepared to do what they do. Since they are prepared they only have to do it, not worry about doing it.

If relaxation is not developed, a comfortable positive attitude remains an illusive dream. The success process cannot be completed.

Emulate a positive person

Another action one might take to continue improving his or her attitude is to emulate positive actions of a person who's respected for having a good attitude and a positive personality. Although personality itself is not the primary motive for trying to improve one's attitude, it's an outward expression of attitude. A friendly personality usually expresses a positive attitude.

While beginning to improve one's attitude by setting clear

goals and learning to be prepared, a person might not know how to express these new positive feelings and emotions. Since many people are recognized for their natural ability to exhibit friendly personalities and positive attitudes, these persons should be used as patterns to emulate. What are some positive characteristics for emulation? These might include:

> Upper body mannerisms - especially hand motions
> Facial expressions
> Voice - tone and inflection
> Diction and clarity of speech
> Timing of expressive participation
> Active listening to other speakers

Naturally, one would not try to emulate another person, exactly. The results of that effort might seem artificial. However, those positive attributes of other people may be used as guides to develop one's own attitude and personality style that's comfortable and positive.

Read self improvement articles

This is easy and simple. One should simply read books and other developmental articles that guide one to a better personality and to better physical health. There are numerous books in bookstores that may guide a person toward improvement in personality, attitude, self confidence, getting along with people, becoming conversationally active, and any other area of concern one might have regarding his or her attitude and personality.

Even if one can't afford to buy books, many are available in libraries. Library books are free, assuming of course they are returned on time.

Avoid anger by empathizing

This action step might be difficult for some people, especially those who feel they must be *right* about everything. Anger or other negative emotional displays tend to cause irrational and illogical perceptions and behavior. These traits certainly don't indicate one has started the day okay with intentions to keep it that way. Neither do anger and high emotions indicate one has learned to relax and expect problems to occur that may be solved. That condition suggests a person is ruled by his or her environment and not in control of it.

Empathy is a positive approach to remain in control of one's emotions and feelings. Empathy means to consider the situation from the other person's point of view. It means to walk in the other person's shoes awhile; to see things from his or her perspective. A person who can empathize is a person who can rationalize to solve problems and answer questions. A person who can empathize learns to focus more on the question or the problem than to focus on protecting a fragile ego or self perceived weakness.

One who can see things and situations from different points of view from a broader perspective is a social person who may become comfortable, confident, and relaxed.

Analyze and reflect

This last step perhaps is the most important, for it incorporates all the other steps to develop a success attitude. At the end of each day one should reserve time to analyze and reflect upon actions and reactions that occurred that day, and to determine what went well and what might have been improved to enhance one's opportunities for success. Basic questions should include:

"Did I remember to start the day okay?"

"Was I prepared for special events today?"
"Was I relaxed most of the day?"
"Did I observe any actions that I should emulate?"
"Did I perform any personal self improvement?"
"Did I become angry or upset? Why?"
"Was I too ego-involved to consider other views?"
"What do I need to improve for tomorrow?"

This reflective exercise should be performed daily until the desired actions and steps become part of one's normal character and personality. When this occurs, one may then feel the creativity of a success attitude. This attitude also gives a clearer understanding to the importance of specific goals.

A powerful success plan begins with clear goals and the right attitude to accomplish those clear goals. Success doesn't just happen, it must be made to happen. Even with a good success plan, however, there are still powerful influences and obstacles. These negative influences must also be understood, for they are powerful enough to defeat even the best success plan. A success plan must have constant support and reassurance.

Determination

Determination is related to one's direct focus and personal pursuit to be successful. Some people interpret this concept of getting ahead as gaining more material possessions. Consequently, their focus may be on getting things, rather than doing things that result in receiving more rewards for work, study, and determination.

Often the despair and futility of trying to get ahead may influence a person to evolve into a problem student and even a problem worker. These problem persons may ordinarily be identified by some of the following characteristics:

The person's performance becomes weak.
The person's attitude becomes disruptive.
The person's actions are more controlled by a peer group.

This misinterpretation of the ideas and conditions of getting ahead, of being successful, is one of their major obstacles to focus and determination. One must remain focused and determined to accomplish actions that result in an evolutionary advancement. To focus only on material possessions and to ignore those methods to achieve those possessions often cause a person to abandon the control he or she has, ultimately and justly, to be rewarded. That ultimate reward will include higher esteem as well as material things.

When one has a good success plan, he or she must prepare to begin those actions. Preparing means to train, to become skilled, and to develop a positive attitude. This may be accomplished by accepting perspectives that might not be part of one's normal culture.

Personal values have an important role that might not ordinarily be considered as a serious success influence. Many beliefs and opinions are reflected as personal values. These values help determine the manner in which a person acts and reacts to work and educational requirements. Those values also often determine that person's attitude toward leadership, the desire for responsibility, his or her confidence level, the degree of involvement, and the eagerness to cooperate.

Students' values in the school environment aren't relevant if they don't conflict with values of that educational environment. If a conflict in values does exist between those students and the environment, those students may become rebellious, experience absences, exhibit low morale, and refuse to become or remain productive.

Sources for developing values include one's close associates and peers, authorities and hero figures, emotional situations, and media communications. Ordinarily, the values and perceptions of a person, including a student, would be the same as those of the person's socioeconomic culture. The strongest influence that helps to develop student values is family culture, family stability, and family support.

Self Improvement

Everyone is for self improvement. No one's ever against it. Most agree self improvement is a good thing everybody should do. They plan to take a course in something, or train in something, to improve themselves. How many people actually follow through on plans to take a course or to begin a training program? Why do those good intentions to pursue one's self improvement rarely develop into action? Why do many fail to do those important things they know they should do? Self improvement should be understood to help reinforce the necessity for personal self improvement and to identify reasons that prevent its occurrence.

Reinforcement to the rewards of self improvement helps one find motivation to begin that important process that ordinarily begins with the first step. Those rewards include enlightenment, graduation, satisfaction, and career advancement.

A constant flow of information is needed for enlightenment. One's mind works at higher efficiency and excitement when it's learning new things it can assimilate. The more information one's mind has, the faster this assimilation process occurs. This is the basis for the narrow view and limited personality of people in the lower social class of society. Their lack of positive self development limits their ability to interpret new information easily and objectively.

There are also many self improvement methods and sources that give a person much satisfaction and joy, including the feelings that Maslow and Herzberg identify as recognition and achievement. That satisfaction often facilitates an attitude that allows one to advance to a higher education or career level.

Avoiding Frustration

A good success plan must also include the ability to solve problems and to face ordinary daily life without yielding to the temptation of becoming frustrated. Everyone's life has many bumpy roads along the way. Ordinarily, it's not the bumpy roads that cause problems. Usually they are caused by the way in which one chooses to travel those roads. Frustration is a normal reaction to many of these bumps of everyday living. Two actions may be taken to learn to face them without the normal reaction of developing frustration.

First, one must have a positive attitude - a success attitude. Some suggestions to develop a success attitude have already been given. Once that success attitude has been developed, a person will possess a trait of self presence. This armor will allow one to accept problems as challenges to be solved rather than as obstacles that are barriers.

Second, one should learn the problem solving process, since those natural road bumps of life are now problems to be solved and not insurmountable barriers. This problem solving process has only six steps:

Identify the real problem - not just the symptoms

Understand the problem - by a full analysis

List alternative solutions

Choose the best solution

Use that solution

Follow-up and evaluate the results

This problem solving process might seem too simple to be a reasonable consideration. It's not. Many problems are never solved because: the real problem is never identified - only a symptom of a problem, some don't consider alternative solutions, and some are afraid of failure - so they don't use any solution.

Improve Communications Skills

To be successful one must learn to communicate well. This is particularly true for students.

Communication requires three abilities. This doesn't include the normal sending, receiving, interpreting and feedback process that's popularly discussed, although these are necessary requirements. These three abilities are: reading, activating communications and communicating effectively:

Reading is the basis for higher learning. A person who cannot read well simply will be handicapped in the learning process. This doesn't mean the person will not be successful, it means the person will not be a positively open person who will reach his or her highest potential. Reading is the exercise that should be given the top priority in any educational environment, including that supervised by a parent at home. *Regardless of the effort required by educational institutions, a student must be taught to read at grade level before advancing to the next grade.*

Many people in our society, including students, are shy, withdrawn or lack confidence, often because they can't read or communicate well. Teachers and parents must recognize these shy symptoms and help children and students overcome these handicaps. If a person is more actively involved in the communications process, that person will more clearly understand reasons and purposes for improving his or her communications skills.

To communicate with purpose, authority, and credibility, one must communicate effectively. This means one must be able to make himself or herself clearly understood, that the communications must be appropriate, and that the grammar in the communications must be adequate to give the speaker credibility.

Communications skills are so important in the general success process they shouldn't be ignored or disregarded at any level of a person's career.

Improving Interpersonal Relationships

Eventually, success must involve other people. It would be rare, indeed, for someone to become successful in a social vacuum. Other people and other people's ideas are important to one's success. For example, in a school environment the relationship between a teacher and a student directly affects the happiness and objectivity of that student.

Three concepts are most important as guiding reminders: 1. Always make the other person feel important. Avoid the personal pronoun, I, as much as possible. 2. There is nothing absolute in life. Everything does not always have a perfectly right and wrong or a true or false answer or reply. Therefore, one doesn't have to win all the arguments to be *more right*. 2. Courtesy is the oil to success. It reduces life's friction.

These success planning concepts, alone, will not assure a person, a student, will be successful. There are many other obstacles and barriers routinely working against one's success plans. One thing is certain, however: *without a success plan to become successful, one has a definite plan to fail.*

How can this success plan be used? It's unlikely young students will understand these concepts by themselves by just reading these words. Parents and teachers are encouraged to formulate these basic concepts within their own frameworks of reference, and to use these concepts consistently and routinely at the best times when their students or children are most receptive.

Furthermore, a class on success planning and personal development should be developed for each school. This would reinforce the concept that success is not something that just happens to a person. It's something one must plan for himself or herself. After all, if the purpose for schools is not to help young people be successful, *why* are schools necessary?

A student needs more than success planning, however, to be successful in school and in the workplace. Certain general work skills are also required. They will be discussed, next.

General Workplace Skills

In addition to teaching students how to learn, how to develop good communications skills, and how to develop a success plan, schools should also teach basic and fundamental workplace skills. These skills would not include those specialized skills ordinarily developed in vocational or job training programs.

School vocational programs were envisioned to fulfill a need in high schools. That idealistic goal was to provide students with the opportunity to plan and train for a career instead of advancing into higher education, for those students who wanted to begin a career. Vocational training hasn't fulfilled its role in the education system due to emphasis and cost. Furthermore, educators, counselors, and parents encourage students to plan for advanced education upon graduation from high school. Society, including educators and parents, suggests anything less implies failure.

General workplace skills training is a more realistic approach. It would also be a more acceptable alternative to parents who want to keep their children from the dark pits of vocational training. General workplace skills would include those universal skills that may be used in various work environments regardless of the specific details of that occupation. These could be conducted in normal schools, without high costs. Some examples include:

Workplace requirements, concepts and terminology

Keyboard skills
Office administration (filing and organizing)
Office equipment operation
Telephone etiquette
Customer service relations
Warehousing concepts and practices
Distribution and shipping techniques
Occupational safety
Security of company assets.

 These are examples of workplace skills and requirements that are applicable to most jobs, but not to one specific occupation. Most jobs require at least some knowledge of each of these functions.
 This training would prepare students to enter most jobs lacking only the technical training of those specific jobs. Most workers who fail at their jobs don't fail from their lack of technical skills. Those who fail, or who become problem workers, do so from their lack of interest, motivation, general job skills, or work ethic. These general job skills would apply to students whether they begin a career as a dropout, as a high school graduate, or after higher education. Employers would be thrilled to know a new employee had enough interest in employment to be prepared with these general and most important skills.

Summary

This approach toward an enhanced education process requires no new education philosophies or ideologies. It may fit comfortably within the current system that, in itself, serves an honorable and high purpose even with its many weaknesses.

Most training and techniques that now exist in the education process are aimed toward directly improving students' knowledge. Nothing substantial could be accomplished without that basic knowledge schools provide. The possible exception is some higher mathematics and literary courses required for graduation for many students who have no need for that advanced knowledge. It destroys their self image and teaches them failure instead of success. However, this question can't be answered until the question regarding the purpose for education is answered. Is it for higher education, for social literacy, for occupations for educators, or to prepare one for a job?

These ideas are to complement that education so it may be used more efficiently. These suggestions are not intended for the purpose of replacing current and classical practices.

On the other hand, school activities designed only to gather information to comply with surveys or to gather data for national education comparisons and statistics should be regarded by our society for what they are. Those activities are disruptive, frustrating for teachers and students, *irrelevant to the purpose of education*, and a serious hint of movement toward socialization of our education systems, and beyond. This is a dangerous activity to our free society, as we now understand what our free and democratic society should be.

School systems must remain under autonomous and local

control, regardless of the differences of some local communities. Variety and discovery concepts are the foundations that protect the free enterprise concepts within our democratic society. Too much centralized power controlling our education system is far more harmful to freedom than a weak; but more open, objective, and applicable approach.

Variety allows the expectation of excellence. Standardization encourages apathy and mediocrity, the great maladies of socialism. One system must not control the thinking of our youth and attempt to socially engineer a new order society. Thomas Jefferson warned of its dangers; and Adolf Hitler, among other tyrants, demonstrated that danger.

For those concerned about racial integration, that provision may still be applied within the concepts of open-market education. Simply follow one of the suggestions by James Coleman. That is to allow any student to attend any school of his or her choice, not allowing any school to reject any applicant. Funding for that student would transfer with the student to the preferred school.

These ideas to help improve communications effectiveness, learning skills, success planning, and general skills are offered to make the current education system really do what it desperately tries to do: to produce students who can contribute to their own welfare and to the welfare of society. Seventy to eighty percent of our students do that now, partially as a result of the current education system. Many of those have innate abilities that would allow them to become successful regardless of any education process.

The other twenty to thirty percent of our students, however, fail to be motivated, inspired, trained, or educated to a level that will bring them into the mainstream of our productive economic society. These students are the 'education dilemma' and are the objects of the ideas and suggestions in this chapter.

Although the education system can create a foundation to help a student become successful, it's not the major success determinant. More important to one's success are one's driving aspirations and motivations, the family, and the influencing culture.

A student reared in a family culture that anticipates, supports, and is accustomed to success will most likely become successful. On the other hand, a student reared in a family culture that has no history of success or that doesn't understand the value of aspirations and effort will most likely not achieve a high level of personal success. Some of those children cultured for failure, however, might find stronger sparks of aspiration and motivation if we show them the face of success. If they understand what success looks like they might not be afraid to reach out further to hold its hand.

The next two parts of this book are designed to help parents offer this essential leadership to help their children succeed. It gives specific information to help their children learn how to learn, and stay in school until they graduate.

Back to School

Chapter 5

TEN PARENTING SKILLS

Some parents who complain most about the poor quality of teachers and the lack of motivation and understanding of students are, themselves, weak in the education process. There probably are some weak and incompetent teachers. There probably are some teachers who are otherwise competent, but who have such personalities that students are afraid to go near their classrooms. Also, many students aren't naturally motivated to use good student skills. They need more encouragement and direction.

These areas in the education system must be considered to help make the education system work effectively. However, these weaknesses cannot be determined until parents have fulfilled their important roles in their children's education. Parents must continue to be involved in the total education process. First, however, they must insure their actions, or lack of actions, give their children a positive attitude to learn rather than a negative attitude toward learning. Parents provide the first level and the first influence to their children's learning. They are the roots to learning. Ordinarily, the teacher's influence is only secondary.

Following are ten teaching skills for parents to help their children learn. Unless the child is naturally gifted, the parent must use these skills to help prepare a child a teacher can teach.

1

Be a Learning Partner

A child should not face the learning process alone. Parents too often fail to help their children learn, for they merely assume the teaching and learning process is a task shared between the school and the child. Perhaps some parents really believe this; others may use this belief as a convenient excuse not to get involved. Furthermore, some parents feel inadequate to help their children with homework and other studies.

Regardless of the reason or the excuse, that reason or that excuse isn't big enough for parents to avoid the responsibility to help their children learn. The parent must be the child's learning partner, regardless of the parent's ability, intelligence, or education level. The parent must participate to provide the child with the confidence, the comfort, the aspirations, the approval, and the safety the child must have to focus on learning. Otherwise, the child will be distracted from learning by focusing on those other missing essentials.

The excuse that many parents use for not helping their

children learn is that they, "Just don't have time." A one parent family often uses that one parent status as a rational justification. Two parent families use the same excuse, "It takes both of us to make a good living, and we just don't have time." Ordinarily, these people who complain most that they don't have time to help their children learn are the same people who complain most about the quality of teachers and schools. It's easier to place the blame on someone else.

Many parents, persuaded by political and social rhetoric, are more strongly supporting the belief that education is the responsibility of schools and teachers. This idea that school systems and teachers are responsible for a child's education is a narrow view of education. Parents must understand the broad view of education to make the learning process work. Education consists of three parts, not just one part or one view, as is generally accepted by those who try to avoid responsibility.

Teaching is only one part of the education process. Schools are responsible for providing facilities and teachers to provide instruction. Schools and teachers are also responsible for creating conditions that will allow student motivation. They are not most responsible for direct student motivation. They are responsible for teaching.

Learning is another part of the education process. Schools and teachers are not responsible for student learning. That process must be accomplished by a student. This student activity, or student involvement, is called 'studying.' A teacher or a school cannot do this function for a student. Studying has no short cuts, nor any quick answers. It must be done, methodically, and by each student, personally and individually.

However, a basic concept of this book is that schools and teachers don't teach students this learning process. The education system, as well as our frustrated society, seems more willing to accept the popular idea that our education problem lies in the lack of quality in our teachers. The acceptable conclusion is that if we have better teachers, we will have better education. Our education system is more focused on teaching than on learning. Since each student must learn - and not teach - learning must be our target to improve education effectiveness. The quality of learning is more important than the quality of teaching. The purpose for this book is to improve that learning quality. Parents are a vital part of that learning process.

Motivation is the third part of learning. The motivation to learn must come from within the child. Neither the parent nor the teacher can 'motivate' a child, or anyone else. A person must be motivated from within. Screaming at a child, offering money and concessions to a child, and giving a motivational speech to a child do not motivate a child. These things might give information to a child to help him or her decide to fulfill a need. Nevertheless, that decision comes from within based upon that child's needs - at that point in time. Most likely, the motivating needs for a child who must endure a critical or condescending motivational lecture from a parent would be simply to escape from that uncomfortable situation.

Parents share in the responsibility to help their children find ways to fulfill their important needs. Through nurturing, loving guidance, and example, a parent must lead the child to feel the needs that are important. Once these needs are felt by a child, the child will create his or her own self motivation to become successful. In this case, successful in making an effort to study and learn.

Parents bring their own children into this world, therefore they are responsible for guiding the development of their children. Schools and teachers are only part of that development. They are not responsible for that development. Parents must be learning partners with their children to guide them through the frustrations, hardships, and difficulties of the learning process.

2

Focus on Effort - Not Grades

Good grades must be considered rewards, not goals. Parents, as well as the education system generally, are narrowly focused on students' grades rather than the process and goals that must be reached to receive good grades. Effort and work are the actions. Grades are the results of those actions. A student cannot make grades. A student can take actions, knowledgeable study, that may produce good grades. An athletic event may be used as an example of this concept.

In a typical athletic event, such as a hundred-yard dash, the runner wants to do his or her best. That person wants to be prepared at the time of the race to do his or her best. To be prepared, that person must be at his or her maximum physical and mental capability at the moment of the race. While preparing to be physically and mentally ready, that person cannot concentrate on the trophy as being the goal. That person must focus on being physically and mentally

Reading Opens Learning Doors

prepared to get to the finish line in the quickest possible time. This preparation must be the goal. If the runner has at least equal ability as other runners and has prepared better, that person will win the race. The trophy for winning will be the reward - not the goal.

Parents, even those with knowledge and good intentions, often focus on the wrong goals when trying to motivate their children to learn. They emphasize grades and not the effort to earn those grades. One question emphasizes this concept: How many parents offer money to their children for grades, instead of time and effort to produce those grades?

3

Keep Communications Open

The basic purpose for a parent is to provide care, training, and guidance for a child. The requirements for physical care are easy to fulfill. A parent understands those physical needs, for we all have the same basic physical needs. Fulfilling emotional and psychological needs requires other considerations.

A child's emotional needs are determined by more subtle factors often hidden by unseen doubts and fears. Each person has his or her individual emotional needs based on his or her life experiences and perceptions. It's unlikely all those experiences and perceptions will be exposed to parents. Often the child does not recognize his or her own emotional needs. These experiences and perceptions must be viewed and understood through open and sincere communications between the parent and child.

Open and sincere communications never develop in some families that allow parents to have a guiding influence over the child's development. Sometimes the parent causes this lack of development; sometimes the child causes the void. In either case the parent is still responsible for bridging the gap to effective communications. In this case, effective communications aren't specified as those that clearly explain but targeted at those the child can understand and relate to his or her perspectives and needs. To reach this relationship the parent must avoid certain barriers to that communication. Some barriers occur naturally, and some barriers are created by parents as they try to influence their children.

One of those barriers is created by the typical admonition, "Why don't you listen to reason; why don't you understand something this simple?" This is a typical comment some parents make in their frustration to 'get through' to their children. The child ordinarily understands the logic being explained, but that logic doesn't fit the child's needs at that time.

Parents create another typical communications barrier when they criticize their children's undesirable friends. Children have the same feelings about friends as adults. They must defend their friends. This is a built-in emotion that cannot be destroyed by logic. In this case, parents must try to fulfill another emotional need of their children to make the attraction to undesirable friends less forceful.

Many children live in homes that don't encourage, or even allow, them to learn open and sincere communications. Some parents are too selfish to consider the emotional needs of their children. They must dominate all the family activity to satisfy their own ego and esteem needs. Some parents don't understand the value of courtesy upon their children's emotional needs. They don't hesitate to scream at their children to, "Shut up!" and then complain to their children that they don't understand.

Other parents simply tell their children they are too young to understand. These are only examples of typical barriers that close communications between parents and children.

Parents must use meaningful communications, not personal frustrations, to learn what their children's immediate needs are. Those needs must be recognized to allow real and open communications. Children's basic needs are the same as adults' basic needs. These include a feeling of belonging and comfort, the desire for respect and love, and the right to feel important. These needs begin when a child understands the concept of the word "I."

4

Schedule Talk Time

Communications must not only be open and sincere, communications must also exist for the parent to have any guiding influence over a child. Too often parents and children are too busy to talk to each other. The lack of communicating creates a habit of not communicating. A habit, once created, is hard to overcome. The time that would ordinarily be taken for talking to each other becomes filled with other essential activity that continues to crowd out time that would otherwise be available for talking.

The habit of not taking time to talk with each other must be broken as any other habit is broken. It takes a concerted effort. Although the concerted effort might seem artificial in the beginning, it must be done. In this case, the habit of not taking time to talk must be replaced by a habit that's more productive. The more productive habit is a scheduled time to talk. Adhering to a schedule, a regularly scheduled time to talk, will force that habit to become as automatic as the habit of not talking.

Each family has its own schedule of times and events. These times and events are determined by ages of family members, location of the home, and family interest in the community. A family with several children who are involved in sports and other activities might have a more difficult challenge finding time for quality conversation than would a family with only one child who's only interested in grades.

Nevertheless, parents must insure quality conversation time exists between themselves and their children. Children must be allowed to learn that good communication skills are important, and parents must allow their children the time and opportunity to express their intelligence, interests, and knowledge. This open expression helps the child develop and reinforce esteem and self-confidence necessary for continuing success.

5

Understand the Learning Process

For most students, grades are determined by the amount and quality of study. Of course, some students are more intelligent than others and make good grades with only little effort. For the average student, however, increased study can offset the small difference in basic intelligence. It's estimated grades are determined approximately sixty percent by intelligence, thirty percent by effort, and ten percent by factors such as random chance.

This conclusion suggests that a student with higher intelligence requires less study time than a student with average intelligence. This conclusion also suggests that a student with only average intelligence can make the same good grades with increased study effort. A student with below average intelligence must make even more effort to make good grades. In either case, study time that reflects that effort must be emphasized more than grades that result from that effort. Frustrated parents often emphasize grades to their children, rather than effort to earn grades.

Those parents typically admonish their children to study harder to make good grades. To study harder suggests or implies the student must somehow find a more focused study method or a more intelligent study method for deeper understanding. This concept gives the impression that the child must become more intelligent to study. This typical admonition to a child creates frustration and despair for that child, for only the same level of intelligence exists. The child can't develop more of it in himself or herself. Within a limited time, intelligence can't be increased. Under this handicap of frustration and despair a student loses confidence and esteem.

    A parent must emphasize increased study time and study skills to a student who needs to improve his or her grades. A student can understand the concept of studying more or learning study skills, but a student - or anyone else - can't understand the concept of studying harder to make better grades. Better grades should be the result of more study time and better study effort by using effective study skills.

6

Know the Teacher

Parents of successful students ordinarily know their children's teachers. Parents of lower achieving students ordinarily don't know their children's teachers. Is there a cause and effect to these relationships? If so, in which direction? Do parents of successful students learn to know their teachers, or, do students become successful because their parents know their teachers well?

Perhaps these relationships are created both ways. Parents of successful students tend to support their children, and want to be recognized for that support. Consequently, they work with teachers to show their level of concern and support for their children. In turn, teachers ordinarily express their appreciation and respect for that parental support. On the other hand, when parents of less successful students work closely with a teacher, that bonding is ordinarily interpreted by students as sincere concern. That concern becomes adopted by the student who recognizes it.

7

Become Involved

Parents who want their children to become concerned and involved with school and education success must demonstrate that concern themselves. Too often, parents use the excuse that they don't have time to be involved in school activities. Too often, also, these are the same parents with failing or low-achieving students.

Although most parents now work at regular jobs, which is the normal reason for not having time to attend school functions, there are functions and activities that may be attended at times parents aren't working. For example, many parent and teacher organizations and associations ordinarily meet in the evenings, not during the normal workday.

Parents must also make time to fulfill their responsibility to their children. That responsibility is to show by example that school is important, and, that to get the most from school the student must also be involved. Parents must show how that involvement affects concern and attitudes. Simply explaining that involvement is important to their children is not enough. A child is more impressed by what happens, not what is said.

8

Teach Positive Self-Esteem

Children are highly impressionable and hear more than some parents imagine. Children's ears are fine-tuned to the extraordinary, and especially to comments about themselves. For example, a parent might be trying to explain a lesson to a young child, and in frustration might exclaim, "This is so simple anybody should understand it." Even a very young child might interpret this unplanned comment as an indication that he or she is less intelligent than most people. The loss of self-esteem and confidence from this interpretation might cause that child to perform at the level that he or she expects; in that lower status.

What should a parent do when facing a tutoring problem that evokes an unplanned destructive statement while trying to do something positive, helping the child? Before trying to help their children with a school problem or homework parents must plan for these frustrations. They will occur.

Children learn many new ideas and concepts. If they already knew them they wouldn't have to learn them. Learning is not always easy. Therefore, the parent shouldn't expect to be successful each time he or she begins a tutoring session. Sometimes it's better to leave the problem for awhile, or get another person with a different perspective to help. Instead of suggesting the child isn't trying to learn or doesn't want to understand, the parent should transfer the child's attention to something easier to learn to help rebuild that lost confidence.

To help avoid frustration, parents must also know that different children learn in different ways. Some children learn through the sense of hearing - by sound. Some learn by sight - by visualization. Still others learn by feel - by touching. Some children are more adept with numbers than with words. Some can learn music with little effort, and some can never learn the concepts of music. Each child is similar, but unique. Each child has an individual and unique quality, and concept of learning. Trying to use the teaching approach that causes frustration often degrades the child's self esteem, which in turn makes learning more difficult.

During the tutoring process, a parent must be prepared for frustration and not let that frustration cause comments that would harm the child's self-esteem and confidence. The parent must also be prepared to teach with the learning approach that best fits the child's learning, whether it's by sound, touch, or sight.

9

Give Books as Gifts

Gifts are important. Gifts from one person to another reflect a transfer of something valuable or meaningful between people. If the person who gives the gift treats that gift as something of value, so will the recipient of that gift. Books, however, are often given without the transfer of a feeling of value. Therefore, they aren't treated as valuable.

When a parent or other relative gives a book to a child for a special occasion, such as a birthday, the book is usually given as a compromise gift, not as a valuable gift. It's not unusual for the person who gives a book to say, "I was going to get you something special, but I found this book I thought you might like." This statement, or similar statements, are interpreted by the average child as meaning, "I thought about getting you something good, but I decided to get you something not good." In this case the book has no value.

Books should be treated as special gifts - for they are special. Books allow a child's mind to play with the thoughts and feelings of other characters. Toys only allow a child's hands, eyes and imagination to play. And, the child's imagination is limited to the concept of the toy.

    Special care must be taken to give value when books are given as gifts, especially to young children. The person who gives a book must give that value by expressing that the book was bought as the perfect gift, not as a compromise gift. The giver of the book must also draw the child into the book by telling the child who the main characters are and what they are trying to do. If the child is not introduced to the characters, he or she might never want to learn more about them.

10

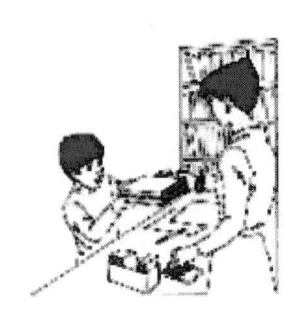

Introduce the Child to the Library

A library is a special place. It's a place where anyone may travel the world, sail all the seas and visit with kings and queens. In a library, a person may participate in a religious feast with a lost native tribe. A person may explore secret caverns and dungeons. And, a person may even rule the world for a few hours. A person may do all these things and many more simply by picking up a different book. And, books are free in a library. A library is the world's best travel bargain.

More than that, a library is the place that proclaims learning, books, and words are important. A library is the place that records history, heritage, and beliefs. A library is the foundation that represents who we are. Libraries are so important that in ancient times they were the first buildings to be destroyed when one city state or one country conquered another.

Chapter 6

TWENTY
STUDENT STUDY SKILLS

Once a student is ready to study and understands the reason for studying, he or she must then get set to study. Getting set requires specific skills and tasks. These skills concern preparing the physical environment for effective study. They and other important study skills will be identified next.

1

Choose a good study area

The first step to create effective study habits is to choose a good study area. Choices in the average home are usually limited to the living room, the kitchen table, a bedroom, or possibly a den.

The location should be a quiet area, such as a bedroom, a den, or study. Trying to create a quiet study area in a routinely noisy area, such as at a kitchen table, is less desirable. In a routinely noisy area, the noise will be anticipated even though it might not be present. Distractions, real or anticipated, are usually magnified for an overly curious child.

The study area should not be so quiet and distant that the child feels isolated or cut off from other people. Although the study area should be relatively quiet, the child should be in an area where he or she may avoid a feeling of isolation.

Lighting conditions are important in the study location.

Generally, indirect lighting is less tiring for reading, assuming the light is bright enough. Enough light, in proper locations, should be provided to prevent glare and shadows on or near the reading material. More than one light might be necessary. A child with tired eyes certainly can't concentrate enough to focus totally on the subject.

Adequate ventilation is also necessary in the study area to allow a student to remain alert. The volume of oxygen is reduced in a closed or unventilated area. A student will not be as alert if the oxygen flow is reduced. This often creates drowsiness and lack of full concentration, which may cause ineffective and wasted study efforts.

2

Prepare the study area

When a student goes to the study area to study, he or she should be prepared to use that time to study. That time shouldn't be wasted searching for materials to help in the study process. Many students use much of their planned study time doing things that are only indirectly associated with studying, not studying. Weak students often use the excuse of looking for things they need to do homework as procrastination to avoid that study and homework. This distraction simply prolongs the anticipated agony of real work and study.

Most items commonly used with study and homework should be located in designated areas - in the designated study area. Some of the most common items are:

Pencils	Pens	Notebook paper
Pencil sharpener	Compass	Protractor
Hole punch	Stapler	Paper clips
File folders	Rubber bands	Hi-lite markers
Dictionary	Thesaurus	Waste basket
Erasers	Alarm clock	Large calendar
Atlas	Ruler	Calculator

Why an alarm clock in the study area? The clock should be set for the planned study time, which will be discussed later. This allows focus on studying, not checking to see how much longer to study.

Fun books, books children enjoy reading, should be in the study area. When studying becomes tiring or tedious, the child can read a fun book to regain reading concentration. Reading without concentration serves no purpose.

A comfortable desk, table, or other flat surface should also be available to write on. A student who writes on a bed, sofa, or in his or her lap often develops sloppy penmanship. This often causes a student to earn bad grades, especially if the teacher can't read that writing.

Although this is a long list, most of these items are already available in most homes. Many of them, however, are moved from place to place and often are hard to find.

3

Set a routine study time

How often do children arrive home from school and announce, "I don't have any homework today?" Or, how often do they say, "I finished my homework at school?" Even worse, how often do they forget to do their homework?

A daily study time, at home, should be set by parents and students, regardless of the amount of homework. This creates a proactive approach to learning. It also indicates an acceptance by students and parents that the student's learning should not be determined only by the effectiveness and performance of the teacher. The child must accept responsibility for learning with the parent as a partner and guide.

Parents and students mutually should set a standard time for study. If more time is needed to complete homework, naturally that time should prevail. If the student has no homework, then he or she should use that time progressively for review, research, or improving other important skills such as reading.

The set study time should not be interpreted by the child as punishment. Talking about that time should be avoided during situations of frustration and stress between the parent and child, especially if that frustration and stress are caused by low grades. The topic should be discussed when the atmosphere is harmonious and friendly, and the conversation is focused on goals, success, and the future.

Study should not be continuous throughout the planned study time. Concentrated study time should be approximately fifteen to twenty minutes with five to ten minute rest intervals. For example, a one-hour study period would result in approximately forty-five minutes of actual study time. This schedule prevents aimless reading and drowsiness, satisfies the child's curiosity of events, and results in more effective study.

Routine and regular study time should be only part of a student's scheduled activities, since a child lives for things other than studying. The child and the parent should make sure time is also scheduled for playing, regular family fun activities, recreational activities, character building, and sleeping. These things are also important to one's development.

4

The parent must participate

Parents should be involved in, and part of, their children's study time and study effort, especially while their children are young. Even if the parent can't help with the actual homework, or doesn't have time to solve complicated math problems, the parent must show positive interest in the study process by asking questions and offering encouragement.

Two ideas are critical to help young children learn to read and enjoy learning to read. First, parents should ask about stories read or introduced in class each day. The child should have an opportunity to show he or she can remember those stories about Dick, Jane, and Spot, or whoever happens to be popular at the time.

Secondly, the parent should listen to the young child read to allow the child to feel important. A child must feel important to develop the necessary self-esteem to succeed.

Of course the approach will be different for older students, for they have different priorities. Although a parent wouldn't ordinarily listen to an older student read, the parent must still provide the interest, encouragement and opportunity for the child's self-esteem.

Research and surveys show that students from homes that have a culture of family participation in the study process are ordinarily more successful. They make better grades, they are happier people, and they tend to be more successful after graduation from school. Some research concludes that a child's grades are more often affected by the level of parental involvement in the study process than by the level of competency of the teacher or the education system.

5

Get enough exercise

Students often fail, or fail to do their best, because they ignore physical demands and physical capacities. Student health plays a major role in student success. It's often ignored, which causes conditions that might be interpreted as lack of motivation, lack of concern, or lack of ability.

Physical exercise is considered the most important health

deficiency of students. Studies indicate the brain works at higher efficiency if it has a good blood supply with plenty of oxygen. A person who doesn't exercise sufficiently deprives his or her brain, and body, of at least some needed oxygen. Authorities suggest as many as forty percent of men students and seventy percent of women students fail to get enough exercise to provide the desired oxygen flow.

Students who appear lazy might not really be lazy; they might be doing the best they can. The best they can do, however, might be limited by the physical and mental deprivation they cause themselves by being too inactive or sedentary. They might be doing their best at that time, but that might not be the best they could do if they were active and healthy.

A student should schedule a time to exercise, with the same emphasis that he or she schedules a time to study. It's not essential it be hard and strenuous. It's not even necessary exercise be scheduled as exercise. Walking briskly is sufficient exercise if it's done routinely. The student may simply accomplish chores and errands by walking instead of riding to a different location to accomplish those tasks.

Younger students, in this age of computer games, often play those games for hours instead of playing in the traditional way that creates natural exercise. This includes running, jumping, climbing, and riding bicycles. Parents should insure their young children don't ignore these normal physical activities that will help keep them healthy. Children should be taught that a well-rounded schedule is healthier than an addiction to one activity.

6

Get enough sleep

Sleep is another important part of studying often overlooked or ignored. It's generally accepted that the average person, especially a younger person, needs at least eight hours sleep each night. Many need more than that, depending upon the person's individual personality and metabolism.

A young person, especially a student, expends much energy during a normal day. Although many students don't get enough physical exercise they still, nevertheless, expend energy. Young children play, which uses energy. Students must read, think, study, and perform in a classroom which also uses energy. Energy may be expended either mentally or physically. Energy is replenished during sleep, assuming of course the person does those other things necessary for health, such as eating the right food in the right amounts.

Sleep also allows other necessary things to happen to a person's body. It allows the body to eliminate toxins that accumulate during the day's activities. It also allows the body to repair itself in those areas where muscle and other tissues are strained or damaged. In summary, the body and the brain are allowed to rest and repair themselves.

The time for sleep must also be considered for sleep to have its best effect. Sleep is more effective if it's done at the same time - and in the same way. If a child is accustomed to going to bed at a certain time, then that time should be maintained as a regular schedule. One's body adjusts to a standard routine. If that routine changes, it takes the body some time to adjust to the new routine. If a person goes to bed at different times, his or her body might never become adjusted, calm, and comfortable. This is the body condition often referred to as 'jet lag.'

Older students should schedule their time for sleep with the same emphasis they schedule their time for study and for recreation. It's part of the over-all schedule, and just as important as any other study skill. Parents of younger children should insure their children develop a good sleep routine.

7

Don't be guided by peer pressure

Peer pressure is an influence that often discourages an otherwise good student from being a good student. Many students who have good intentions to study often are discouraged by pressure from their peers. Ordinarily, it's easy for most students to be influenced by their friends. They like their friends, they like to be around their friends, and they're comfortable with their friends. Unfortunately, negative peer pressure as well as positive peer pressure comes from one's friends. Only friends can use peer pressure. Who could be pressured by someone they didn't like into doing something they didn't want to do? Acquaintances who are disliked have no influence over a person.

How and why is peer pressure so powerful that it often replaces logic? Why is it so powerful that a person will often do something he or she knows is not the right thing to do? Peer pressure is powerful because it acts to fill basic needs that influence people.

According to motivation theories, people like to feel safe; they like to feel they belong to something important; and they like to feel respected. These likes are really needs. They need to feel safe. They need to feel they belong to something important. They need to feel respected, which creates a feeling of esteem.

Some peer pressure is positive, especially if the student is in a group with high ideals and high expectations of success. As a member of this group, a student tries to comply with the normal expectations (norms) of the group. These positive norms are respect for good grades, courtesy, understanding, and respect for each other's success.

A student who's part of a group with low ideals, low aspirations, and low self-esteem will most likely be influenced to comply with negative norms. In this negative group, a student who would mention success would be called a 'snob.' A student who attempts to make good grades would be branded a 'bookworm.' A student who tries to be respectful and courteous would be labeled a 'sissy.' A low-esteem group conditions and forces otherwise successful students to be low-achieving students.

Students with high potential and high ideals often trap themselves in negative groups that offer nothing but pressure to fail. This entrapment happens subtly and slowly. There are no bells, signs, or signals that announce: "You are now entering the influences of a low-esteem and negative group."

To remain free from the influences of a negative reference group, or low-esteem peer group, a student must make a positive and conscious effort to understand how negative peer pressure attacks a rational person, and how to avoid it. A student who's not alert might be drawn into the pits of negative peer pressure by a good friend.

The best way to avoid negative peer pressure is to develop a positive success plan and remain focused. Focusing on that goal will overcome most obstacles and distractions.

8

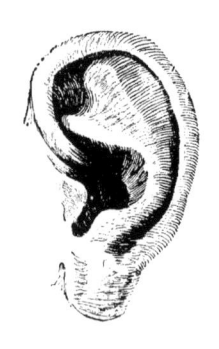

Learn to listen

Effective listening is a learned skill. It doesn't just happen. This is especially true in an environment where new concepts and ideas are introduced, such as in a school environment. In this environment, each word and each phrase are important to meaning and understanding.

Is listening easy? Is there no work to listening? Do you just let it happen? It's not easy; and there's lots of work to it. Let's explore some of the major problems that cause effective listening to be difficult.

It's not unusual for someone to drift off into nice thoughts and experience daydreams. Often a person daydreams when he or she is 'listening' to someone. It would be rare if that person could listen with understanding if his or her thoughts were focused in another area. To listen with understanding - the purpose for listening - one must not only hear those spoken words, one must also actively identify and interpret each word or thought.

A person's opinion of the speaker often influences effective listening. One who listens to a friend, or to someone he or she likes, will be more open and receptive to those words and ideas. One who must listen to someone who's disliked, or someone who causes frustration, will often ignore the meaning of important words from that person. For example, it might be difficult for a student to concentrate on information given by a teacher he or she dislikes. That might cause those words to have less meaning and validity.

Another example is the relationship between the teacher and the parent. If the parent likes the teacher, the parent will be more inclined to listen to the teacher's suggestions for helping a child study. If a parent doesn't like or trust the teacher, the child's low grades will more likely be attributed to the bad teacher. The parent might regard a teacher's instructions as excuses and self-justifications.

Teacher's also have their biases. Perhaps they don't listen to a child or his or her parents because the child is regarded as an undesirable or a trouble-maker with bad parents who don't care. In many cases the child might suffer from an emotional disorder or an attention disorder, which makes positive listening difficult. Good communications must exist in all areas associated with a student for a student to gain the most from studying. The student must listen, with meaning, to learn. Parents and teachers must also really listen to help with that student's learning process.

9

Learn to take notes

    Some students think they can remember what the teacher says in class. They feel they are intelligent and have good memories. Consequently, those students think it's a waste of time and effort to take notes. Students should know why it's important to take notes, how to take notes, and how to use those notes. Parents and teachers must be prepared to teach young students how to take and use notes.

    Learning, especially for class work, is basically an exercise in remembering. A student must learn to remember basic facts and ideas before he or she can use those basics to form concepts and higher ideas. Remembering has a certain reinforcement schedule.

    Ordinarily, something initially learned is forgotten in the first eight hours. It's forgotten, unless it has reinforcement. After only one positive reinforcement event, that fact or idea might not be forgotten for thirty days or longer. Another reinforcement event might make the memory last for several months. Of course the point is reached where additional reinforcement adds no significant value to memory.

Notes make reinforcement of memory easy and convenient. If a student takes notes during a lecture or discussion, that student doesn't have to try to remember and recall the complete lecture. If a student doesn't take notes, and the same information is not in a book, chances are the student will not remember any part of the lecture the next day unless the teacher reviews that lecture. The student must take notes, for the teacher might not repeat and review that same information.

Note-taking in class should be simple enough to allow the student to listen to the teacher while writing notes. If the student is concentrating on taking such thorough notes that he or she doesn't understand the lesson, the student might miss other important concepts and information. Notes taken during a lecture should be words or phrases that identify important information.

The student must organize his or her notes as soon as possible, preferably within a few hours. Remember, after eight hours most memory is lost if it's not reinforced. While the student is expanding those notes, he or she should also recall other information the teacher emphasized and add that to the notes. Revised notes should be complete, but they should also be condensed. A student who tries to write too many notes will use valuable time that might be used better for another subject. Revised notes should have space to add additional comments as they are remembered when the student reviews those notes.

In summary, the student should routinely review notes. The first review must be within a few hours, before the most important information is forgotten. The second review may be after a longer period. Further review depends upon how well the student remembers the material during his or her review. Once the material is learned there's no reason to over learn. That time might be needed to study another subject, or to organize notes from another class.

The student must not wait until the night before a test to review notes. The normal learning curve will not allow necessary memory reinforcement.

10

Learn to outline or hi-lite

Students often open a book, read its words, then close it without remembering what the first paragraph said. When they read the book later as a review or to study for a test, they don't review, they must read as though they had never read the material before, especially if they were daydreaming when they read it the first time.

A student who outlines or hi-lites reading material improves his or her learning skills and makes the review phase faster, easier and simpler. Two learning concepts help make these actions more effective studying.

First, if a student prepares an outline, that student is really organizing ideas. To organize ideas one must be alert and thinking. It's difficult to let one's mind daydream if that person is really active in the reading-organizing process. It gets the person actively involved in the message instead of merely letting his or her eyes see random words.

Secondly, a student who outlines adds reinforcement to the message. Reading the material is the first action, and writing the note is the second action which is reinforcement. It's easier to remember if an idea or a fact has reinforcement.

Outlining is more effective than hi-liting or underlining in a book, although hi-liting or underlining is better than neither. Hi-liting serves the same purposes as outlining. It occupies the reader's mind and provides reinforcement, for a student will usually give some second thought to decide what to hi-lite or underline.

Outlining and hi-liting offer another great advantage. If a student becomes skilled at outlining or hi-liting, the review process becomes quicker and easier. The student doesn't have to keep reading the complete material to review and prepare for tests. He or she simply studies the condensed material, with an occasional overview of the full material to insure no important points were missed.

Although it's easier to underline and hi-lite in a book or other study material, a student must learn to outline from those study references. Some books are loaned and students aren't allowed to mark in them. In this case, outlining is the only practical answer to easy study. Outlining also allows the student to put related and similar information in the same group for better understanding.

11

Use flash cards

Using flash cards is a proven study skill, especially for younger students. Young children usually have shorter attention spans. They concentrate on something for a short time and then lose interest. Flash cards create the idea of a game, which is more fun than studying. They also fit into the short attention span of a young child. Each new flash card is a new subject to attract his or her interest.

For young children flash cards should be simple and convey only one bit of information. For example, flash cards for addition problems should have only one question and one answer on each card. Flash cards can be made on standard index cards or any other standard paper that's easy to handle. Parents should always help their young children with flash cards. Parents' involvement helps keep the child's interest focused on the importance of study time. It also helps to establish discipline in the study process.

Flash cards may also be used effectively for older students. An older student would more likely consider them note cards instead of flash cards.

Older students should have note cards for important concepts and ideas a teacher might ask on a test. They should also have note cards for standard formulas and equations that must be memorized to solve mathematical problems. Anything that pertains to a definite concept or something that must be memorized should be on a note card.

Older students should have their important note cards with them at all times. It doesn't matter if they get bent and crinkled in one's pocket. The service they provide is more important than how they look. They should be used anytime a student is waiting for something to happen or looking for something to do. Students will be surprised how much time they spend just waiting. They should use their flash/note cards during these waiting periods,

## 12

Improve reading skills

A student often misses key ideas and facts while studying, not because the student isn't smart, but because the student doesn't understand how to read effectively. Usually, a student who reads words slowly and carefully is concentrating on words and not thoughts and ideas those words create. Thoughts must be understood to make sense from reading. One who doesn't know how to identify those thought signals cannot make the best use of study time.

Books and other reading material have signals that tell the reader which words and thoughts are important and which are support material, definition material, or explanation material. Some signals are determined by their location in the writing and some are determined by preparatory words.

Most study and homework are from textbooks. Most textbooks are written in the common format of chapters, paragraphs, and sentences. If a student understands how these segments are arranged,

Reading Opens Learning Doors

he or she may learn to pick out the key points from other support information.

Book chapters are divided into paragraphs. Ordinarily, the first paragraph in each chapter tells what the chapter is about. This gives a clue to the important points in the chapter. The last paragraph often summarizes the important information in the chapter. It should reinforce the first paragraph. Before reading a chapter, the student should read and understand the first and last paragraphs. That understanding will make the chapter have more meaning.

Paragraphs usually have signals that alert readers to the main points. These are in the form of topic sentences. Topic sentences are usually first in the paragraph, but not necessarily. Often, the first sentence is an introduction to the topic sentence. Topic sentences are easy to recognize after only a little practice. A student must know they exist, however, to learn how to recognize them.

Individual sentences also have signals that say, 'Okay, here comes an important point - pay attention.' These signals are special words such as: now, therefore, however, except, greatest, important event, at this time, currently, solution, idea and theory. Many others exist and may be identified merely by looking for them.

Students often have an assignment to read only part of a chapter. When this happens the student should also read the first and last paragraphs. It reminds the student what the chapter is about, and the purpose for that reading.

A student should never read assigned homework without having a dictionary within easy reach. Children will often skip over a word they don't understand, and it might be the most important word in the reading assignment. If it's an unusual word it will most likely be a word used in a test. A student should automatically learn the definition to any word that he or she doesn't understand. If a dictionary isn't nearby, that word might remain a mystery to the student.

13

Use a timer while studying

If a student plans to study for an hour, he or she shouldn't spend much of that hour watching a clock to see how much longer to study. A student's mind must be focused on a subject to get the most from study time.

Five minutes of focused and concentrated study is better than an hour of studying while wondering about the time. It's difficult to interpret ideas, meanings, and concepts while reading if one wonders how much longer to study. Ordinarily, if the interest is split while reading, the reader sees only words, not ideas. The purpose for study is to remember important ideas. A timer allows one to concentrate on his or her studies.

14

Create a good environment

The quality of a student's home environment directly affects the ability, the interest, and the motivation for a student to study and to learn. Everyone in the home is responsible for the quality of life in that home to create those conditions that allow effective study.

The student must consider himself or herself a vital part of the family. As such, the student is as responsible for conditions in the home environment as any other member of the family. Those conditions must be supportive and harmonious to allow and encourage positive actions by all members of the family; not a negative environment that creates discouragement and despair.

Parents must be the leaders in the home to set the example of a comfortable home environment. In many cases the example the parent sets is the only condition children understand. If a parent is autocratic, domineering, and unreasonable, the child will assume that's normal for a family environment. That is until the child visits families of friends who live in homes with more love and understanding.

A home environment that's ruled by loud voices, defensive justifications, threats, violence, and the unending effort to prove oneself 'right' will be focused on personality and meaningless trivia rather than on progress and meaningful goals. A child's personality and interests will be handicapped in such a negative environment.

Parents must be aware of this handicap they place on their children if they don't maintain an atmosphere in the home that will allow the student to focus on study, grades, and meaningful success. It's not unusual for the parent who screams loudest at their children for making bad grades to be the source of those bad grades by the ringing of those screams in the child's head. It's not unusual for the parent who condemns teachers most harshly for causing their children not to learn properly to prevent that learning by their harshness that distracts from that positive learning. It's just as common for some parents to blame their children for lack of interest and concern about grades when those parents never offer to help their children with homework or to prepare for a test.

A young student will have no defenses against the ravages of an unhealthy home environment. Some young students may be successful because they like their teachers, because that's simply their natural personality, or because they have good friends who make good grades.

Older students have options once they know the home environment might contribute to their inability to focus on real and positive learning. They may try to explain the problem in the family; which might not have positive effects, for a defensive and autocratic parent would not accept the possibility that he or she could be the cause. They may find a location outside the home to study, at a routine time. The best solution, if possible, is to become part of a study group that's concerned about grades and personal success.

Teachers ordinarily recognize students who are performing at less than their reasonable ability; but the cause of that deficiency is often attributed to low motivation. Low motivation always has a cause.

A negative home environment is one of those major causes. A teacher who recognizes or suspects a negative home environment as the source of a student's despair and low grades should encourage that student to find a friendly study location, perhaps the library, or to join a friendly and progressive study group.

Students and parents aren't the only people in homes who cause or create negative environments. Siblings often create that conflict and turmoil. It's the parents' duty to control those siblings to allow a child time to study without interference.

15

Choose successful friends

One's friends often determine the attitude that person will develop. Although another study skill cautioned about the influence of negative peer pressure, there's another influence that develops without pressure. That involves self-image and self-expectations. A person who thinks well of himself or herself, one who has real self-esteem, will become comfortable with other people who share those same traits.

There's an old saying, 'Birds of a feather flock together.' In applying this saying to people suggests those who regard themselves as successful, worthy, positive, and self-aware prefer to be with other people who share those same qualities. In school, these are ordinarily the students who respect themselves and other people, they have their homework prepared, they cooperate with teachers and administrators, and they participate in positive group activities.

There ordinarily are two other identifiable groups in schools. Those who flock together with negative attitudes and low self-esteem, and those who isolate themselves to remain alone, probably also from low self-esteem and insecurity. The student who remains alone may be driven to good grades to compensate for that loneliness and that feeling of insecurity. Even with good grades, however, that person remains handicapped in the success process, for a person ordinarily must know how to interact with other people to be successful.

The group that flocks together from common negative characteristics reinforces negative expectations within the group, even without peer pressure. Within that social cluster, low performance, low expectations, and low aspirations are the norms. Being successful is considered an alien condition that exists in other groups.

The positive group will say:

"When are we going to do that?"
"Do you want the homework typed or handwritten?"
"Let's get together after school and study math."
"What club or school activity do you belong to?"

The negative group will say:

"Do we really have to do that?"

"Do we have to turn in homework?"
"Let's leave school early today, or just skip."
"I stay away from all those clubs."

A positive student should become part of that positive group or, at minimum, feel that he or she is part of the positive group. This creates a feeling of normal success that makes study seem more natural.

16

Set realistic goals

Study goals should be reasonable and realistic. A student who routinely makes D and C grades shouldn't plan to make all A grades on the next report card. Although that might be possible, if the student had been a real slacker, it's not a practical approach. The student should plan to make some improvement, but not necessarily to take a giant step. The parent must be just as patient.

A student must change many things to improve his or her grades. All those things cannot be changed immediately. Study time must increase, without causing the student to become tired and weary. This includes a learning and adaptation process. Adjusting to a new study location takes time. Changing one's attitude about himself or herself takes time. One doesn't immediately change a negative self-image into a positive self-image without many 'little wins' along the way to keep that positive self-image growing. Long trips are taken with single small steps. Learning to improve grades requires that same approach. The good part, however, is that any improvement is positive improvement and reinforces the learning process.

One grade reporting cycle might not be enough to create any visible grade improvement for a student who starts with no disciplined study skills. At that time much of the focus of the student will be on the system and the method, not necessarily on effective study. There's also the possibility the next grade reporting cycle or test cycle might cover material that's unusually difficult.

Although earning good grades is important, in the beginning a student must focus more on the discipline of study than on the results of study. The student can control the discipline of study but not necessarily the results. Results will eventually occur when the student learns the process and the discipline. Ordinarily, the only difference between a C grade and a B grade is simply a little more effective study time.

Students and parents must also remember that grades may improve without that improvement being visible on a report card. For example, a grade of C might be earned with a grade average of 70 through 80. A student who improves his or her average from 70 to 80 makes a significant improvement. That should be considered one of the 'little wins' to add reinforcement and encouragement to keep improving.

Goals must be set high enough to offer a challenge and encouragement. They shouldn't be set so high they create defeat and lost aspirations. They often create worse despair if they can't be achieved.

17

Trust yourself and like yourself

Self-confidence, self-esteem, and success are things that grow together to become mutually supportive. A person who's successful will have self-confidence and self-esteem. A person who's confident will usually be successful and be proud of that success. A person who values personal pride and esteem will ordinarily be successful and confident. Since these traits accompany each other, a student may begin a good study skills program by focusing on either trait.

When first beginning to learn good study skills positive results might not begin immediately. It might take some time to learn those skills. Learning study skills is similar to learning anything else. One doesn't become a skilled ice-skater with just one lesson. That takes years. One doesn't become a professional basketball player by knowing how to bounce a basketball. That takes years of practice. One doesn't become an effective public speaker by being able to talk. That also takes knowledge and practice, including a combination of acceptable personality traits.

People become proficient in something in large part because they like themselves and they trust themselves and their dedication. A person who wants to become a professional ice-skater doesn't become discouraged and quit with the first fall, or the second, or the third. That person falls hundreds of times but never gives up. A basketball player doesn't quit when he or she misses a shot, or a thousand shots. The self-confidence keeps that person practicing one more time. A public speaker doesn't quit the first time he or she forgets a quote or becomes embarrassed before a crowd. That speaker does it one more time until it becomes natural. These winners have two special traits. They like themselves and they trust themselves.

Becoming a good student, learning good study skills, requires the same traits and dedication as becoming effective in any other facet of life. A student who likes himself or herself and who trusts himself or herself will not become discouraged and quit trying after the first fall or the first miss. That student will have the courage and dedication to try one more time.

In his book, *The Power of Positive Thinking*, Norman Vincent Peale advises, "When tackling a problem the number one thing is, never quit attacking it." Robert Schuller advises in his book, *Possibility Thinking*, "Great people are just ordinary people with an extraordinary amount of determination."

18

Don't be afraid to ask for help

Many people, including students, are afraid to ask a question or to ask for help. They don't like to ask questions for different reasons, which include:

1. They are too shy to ask.
2. They don't know how to ask the question.
3. They don't like the person they must ask.
4. They think it will make them look stupid.
5. They think the other person dislikes them.
6. They think the question isn't important.

Asking questions serves two valuable purposes. First is the obvious purpose; it creates answers to questions. If a question exists, then it's important to someone to have the answer. This is particularly valuable for a student, for one question might provide the clue to many answers.

Secondly, asking questions forces a person to interact with other people; which is itself a valuable experience. In his book, *Our Troubled Selves*, Allan Fromme writes, "Alone, we think less of ourselves, for sooner or later we feel rejected." He states further, "Separation from people usually becomes painful."

A student should try to find answers and solve problems by himself or herself; but that effort shouldn't become so laborious that it turns to frustration and despair. That feeling defeats the learning approach.

If possible, the student should ask the question to the teacher who teaches the subject that has the difficult question. Often, however, the student might not be comfortable talking with that teacher. In that case the student should discuss the question with another teacher, or with a student who most probably knows the answer. Most people like to be asked questions, if it's on a subject they understand. Recognizing their knowledge and ability is a compliment to them.

19

Learn how to take tests

A student should understand what tests are and how to take them before he or she begins to take tests. One should become test-wise in the art of testmanship. If not, that student is not prepared to do his or her best. Only a brief summary of testmanship skills will be identified here. Books are available in bookstores and libraries that give more in-depth details. Key points to taking tests include:

Review test material before the test. If the student has developed good study skills, most information will already have been learned. A review before the test, however, is necessary to test the student's memory and to reinforce important specific facts. Pay close attention to topic sentences in the basic reading material, and compare those to notes, outlines, and flash cards.

Get enough rest and sleep the night before the test. A tired mind and body are less likely to allow information to be recalled. Some tests, themselves, are physically and mentally tiring.

Understand the instructions. In the lower grades these instructions will normally be given orally by the teacher. In the higher grades, the instructions are often written at the beginning of the test. In either case, those instructions must be understood to insure questions are answered in the right manner and order, and not in reverse. Understanding the testing process is as important as knowing the answers.

Know how much time is allowed for the test. Scan through the test material to see how much time may be allowed for each section, or part. Will more time be needed for essay questions, or does the test require only choice answers?

Stay alert to key words in the test. For example, true-false tests often give clues to answers by words such as always, never, all and none. If you must guess for a true-false answer, the answer should be your strongest first impression, or 'false.'

Answer the easy questions first. This serves two purposes. First, the student knows how much time he or she has left to consider the difficult questions. Easy questions will not be left unanswered if there's not enough time to complete the test. Secondly, answering the easy questions first often provides information or clues to answer the more difficult questions. Work on the more difficult questions next. Don't use too much time thinking about the same question, unless it's the last question.

Understand the different types of tests. These include:

* **True-false**

* **Multiple choice**
* **Matching**
* **Fill in the blanks**
* **Essay**

    Each type of test has its special character that must be learned. As stated above, true-false tests have exclusionary words that suggest a false answer. Multiple choice questions usually have two answers that are clearly wrong. Matching questions usually have the same number of questions as answers. If one doesn't fit at the end, then one or more of the answered questions must be wrong. A fill in the blank question might give clues from other questions. Essay questions usually ask the student to inform, describe, explain or justify. The student must know the different meanings of these words. Books are available in libraries and bookstores that explain these different tests in more detail.

20

Reward yourself

Good things should be reinforced to make them happen again. This is a process called *positive reinforcement*. Although positive reinforcement is normally used incorrectly and abused, it should be used to enhance learning skills.

Positive reinforcement often is attempted by parents who promise to pay their children money for making good grades. This system seldom works because the money is a promise and becomes an indebtedness if the child improves his or her grades. It's not a reinforcing reward. For effective reinforcement the reward should be given by the parent, or teacher, after the good performance, without specifically applying that reward to that performance. The child must be allowed to make that association by himself or herself. That association of action and results, not the promise of a reward, creates the reinforcement.

On the other hand, the child should openly celebrate and reward himself or herself for hard work and sincere efforts. If the student is an older child, perhaps he or she should treat himself or herself to a special movie, a party, or an extra large banana split. For the younger child, perhaps a trip to the zoo or a nearby fishing hole would be appropriate.

In any event, the reward should be based on hard work, effort, and sincerity, not necessarily grades. Good grades are only the result of that effort. If a child works hard to learn good study skills and doesn't make better grades on the next test, that effort should still be rewarded. Good grades will eventually occur if the student doesn't become handicapped by disappointment and despair.

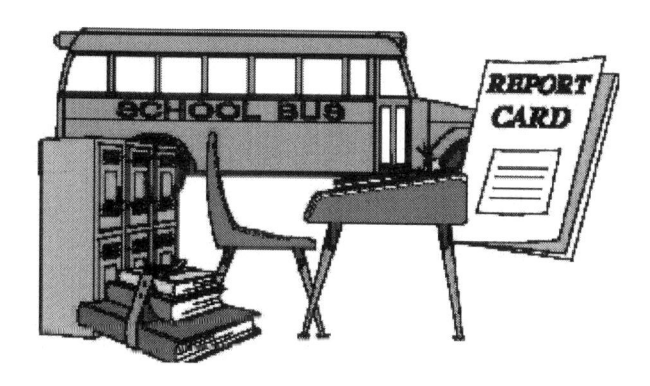

REVIEW

A student will not know the results of his or her efforts to use good study skills until after the real test. That real test includes homework and examinations.

Perhaps the student will learn to use good study skills quickly, or perhaps the student might need a little more time and concentration. In either case, the student must continue to review his or her efforts to determine what he or she is doing right or wrong. The self-review process must continue. One can always do something better, or if not better at least easier.

Questions that one might ask during this self-analysis include:

1. Do I really understand these study skills?
2. Do I spend enough time really studying?
3. Am I serious, or only pretending to study?
4. Do I really want to make good grades?
5. Are my friends too important to me?
6. Do I have too much idle time?
7. Am I comfortable in my study location?
8. Do I ask for help when I need it?
9. Do my friends make good grades or bad grades?
10. Do I know how to read effectively?

Answers to these questions will often explain to a student or the parent why these study skills aren't working. Once the reasons are understood, they may be corrected.

A Success Story

Born into total poverty, this child was destined to fail in life's economic struggle. His father was an alcoholic who abandoned the family when the child was four years old. His mother never graduated from grammar school, and had no career skills other than manual labor. The place was the red clay hills in central Mississippi. The time was 1943, at the height of World War Two when basic necessities were scarce, especially for the poorest people.

Fortunately, or unfortunately as the case may be, women were suddenly in demand for hard backbreaking jobs that previously had been available only for men. Most young men were in jobs contributing directly to the war effort, so women were welcomed into the civilian workforce to fulfill those worker requirements. The mother, too proud to accept welfare assistance, moved to Pascagoula, Mississippi, to become a welder at the Ingalls Shipbuilding Company.

Their home in Pascagoula was a thirty-foot house trailer that was part of a temporary trailer compound located on Mantou Street. Bathroom facilities were located in the center of the compound. The first movie the child saw was from an outside projector flashing onto a bed sheet hung from the common bathroom building. It was a western, starring Lash Larue. The first time he heard *Rudolph The Red-Nosed Reindeer,* by Gene Autry, was in a little café on the corner of Mantou Street and Ingalls Boulevard. They survived: the mother, the four-year-old child, and a two-year-old brother.

When the war ended, in 1945, they migrated back to the red clay hills in central Mississippi. For several months the family lived in a three-room shack. Old newspaper from trash bins was a valuable resource there, for it was used as insulation to keep the winter wind from blowing through the gaps in the unpainted and unfinished oak boards on the outside of the framed structure. There were no inside

Reading Opens Learning Doors

walls or inside insulation. The shack was heated by a small pot-belly, wood-burning heater in the central room and a wood-burning stove in the kitchen. That shack collapsed two years after the family moved to another location.

The mother started working at a shirt factory for minimum wage. She quickly gained a reputation as a hard-working, dedicated, and totally honest person. Although her pay was only seventy-five cents an hour, the local bank loaned her three thousand dollars to buy a ten-acre farm that had an old house on it. The house was in barely livable condition, but it was a home and it would be repaired to be a real home. The mother wanted her two children to have a permanent, stable home so they could be educated in a secure environment. The child was now six years old and, as any normal six-year old, was excited about starting school.

This home was also heated by a wood-burning stove and a fireplace. The out-house was really outside, fifty yards behind the house. Lighting was from kerosene lamps and candles, for there was no electricity. Water was drawn with a rope and pulley from a fifty-foot deep well. Frequently, during the summer months, salt was thrown into the well to kill mosquito larvae, locally called *wiggle-tails*.

The farm, ten acres of scrub land, was gully-washed and greatly endowed with an innocent looking yellow-flowering plant called a *bitterweed*. The farm cow, Bossy, had a constant diet of those weeds, along with the few good bites of grass she could find.

Breakfast for the family was a mixture of butter and molasses stirred together, and eaten by dipping homemade sopping biscuits. Lunch and supper for the family was usually cornbread crumbled into a glass of milk and eaten with a spoon. The milk was bitter from the weeds Bossy ate. The cornbread often had large husks, not sifted out at the local grist mill. Bossy wore out and died eight years later.

The family had a special treat on most Friday nights. It was either fried chicken or bologna sandwiches. Sometimes they even had a bag of Oreo cookies or a box of vanilla wafers.

First grade was so exciting for that six-year-old. There were

Reading Opens Learning Doors

new boys and girls to play with. The exuberance and anticipation of learning to add and subtract, to read real words, to tell time from a clock, and to learn about the sun, the moon, and dinosaurs, were almost overwhelming. He was awed by the fantastic new and tremendous world. Glowing with excitement he could hardly wait for morning to start each school day.

A whole new world evolved for the boy during the first three school years. Not only did he learn reading, writing, and arithmetic, he also began to understand the reality of the differences between economic and social classes. He discovered questions, such as: Why am I the only one with holes in the knees of my pants? Why do I have a peanut butter sandwich for lunch, everyday?

When he was in the third grade the world crushed down upon him even further. He realized he could not talk and communicate like everyone else; he was a stutterer. He was totally devastated, constantly embarrassed, and had no place to hide. Ridicule, embarrassment, terror, and panic were everywhere. The harder he tried not to stutter, the worse his handicap became. It dominated every event and action of his life.

His teenage years were a constant series of panics and withdrawals. Class recitals and verbal questions from teachers made his heart rush to his throat, and caused his clothes to become soaked with perspiration. Usually, he had to decide between the choices of looking stupid by saying he didn't know the answer to the question, or of looking ridiculous by trying to give an answer to the question. He knew he could never get the right words from his mouth. He usually chose to look stupid by responding, "I don't know," to those classroom questions.

He enjoyed being around people, especially small groups. He knew individuals in small groups were usually considerate of the other people's feelings and wouldn't laugh and ridicule as would people in larger groups. He avoided large groups whenever possible. On those occasions when it was impossible to avoid being part of a large group, he was an inconspicuous non-participant. He had learned that a hidden compelling force existed in large groups that made people, even close friends, do or say harsh things they would never do or say on a closer personal level. Although he didn't know the name of that force, he had identified the peer pressure monster at an early age.

The most tragic event happened when he was fifteen. His closest friend, a friend for nine years, didn't invite him to his birthday party. It was inconceivable. There were tears and disbelief. He tried to imagine that his friend had forgot to invite him. He tried to imagine that his friend assumed that he knew he was invited. He wondered if he should ask - but he knew he wasn't invited, and he knew why.

The withdrawal became deeper. Surprisingly, to himself, the withdrawal was not from a feeling of anger or a sense of rejection. He realized the withdrawal from his friendships was to protect his friends from the embarrassment of associating with or being in the uncomfortable environment of a severe stutterer. Each stuttering occurrence was tense, embarrassing, and humiliating for everyone present.

Stuttering is a special problem, for it happens unexpectedly and doesn't permit listeners time to consider how to react. There's no way for a stutterer or the listener to find a mutually comfortable reaction when stuttering occurs, even when it's anticipated. He realized these were difficult times for his teenage friends, anyway, since these were the difficult years, so he often avoided close friendships and associations. His feeling was that his problem was a personal one. He would either overcome it by himself, or suffer the consequences by himself.

He got a summer job when he was seventeen. His uncle hired him to cut pulpwood. Pulpwood is from pine logs, cut into segments, measured by the cord, and used to make paper products. He worked twelve hours a day, six days a week. He was paid a dollar a cord, and usually earned twenty-five to thirty-five dollars a week. He returned to his last year of high school understanding the value of getting his high school diploma.

He had two significant high points during his last year in high

Reading Opens Learning Doors

school. First, he realized his intelligence level was average. He learned that if he studied he could improve his grades. He graduated with a grade exactly in the middle of his class grades. Secondly, he finally got a date with a girl. He took her to the movie, had popcorn and a coke, and took her home. It was excitement beyond imagination. He had become a normal person.

He graduated from high school in 1957, the first in his extended family to reach that goal. Finally, he had made it. Two things had kept him going to school and facing each humiliating and embarrassing moment until graduation. One was the unwavering encouragement his mother gave him about the importance of a high school diploma. The other was the idea that he could face the embarrassment and emotional trauma of being a stutterer, but the idea of being a quitter would have been intolerable. Pride and desire were too strong to tolerate quitting.

The first giant step had been taken; he had earned a high school diploma like other normal people. Now, the next step in real life was ahead. He must venture into the real world and get a job. He wondered how he could do that, when usually he couldn't even ask a complete question or carry on a regular conversation. Even worse, saying his own name was the most difficult task. He realized one must introduce himself or herself when asking for a job, or for an application for a job.

As a simple solution to that problem he decided to join the U.S. Air Force. He knew there would be no job interview to join the Air Force. One became an applicant for the military service merely by walking into the recruiting office. It was almost that simple, since recruiters were that anxious to have another volunteer. Four days after he graduated from high school he was in basic training at Lackland Air Force Base in San Antonio, Texas.

Basic training was relatively easy, and lasted only eight weeks. Only a little interpersonal communication was required, because most training activities and events were done in group formations, where individuals were generally obscure. Little verbal communication was required, other than, "Present, Yes sir, and No sir." Even slurring those easy words was accepted as military jargon. He remained at Lackland Air Force Base another twelve weeks to complete Basic Hospital Corpsman School. Then he was transferred to the Great Lakes Naval Training Center, in North Chicago, Illinois, to complete sixteen more weeks of advanced Hospital Corpsman School.

A whole new world had opened for this young man. The military training had already instilled several key success concepts in him. Most important were the concepts of goal orientation, personal initiative, and confidence. During the sixteen weeks of hospital school at Great Lakes Naval Training Center he completed the course as an honor graduate while he also completed tests which earned college credits. For being an honor graduate he was allowed to select his next assignment location. He chose to return to Mississippi, at Keesler Air Force Base, in Biloxi.

Real life returned during his job placement interview at the Keesler hospital. Since he still had great difficulty talking, he and the job placement counselor agreed he should be assigned to a job with only minimum verbal requirements. He was assigned to Central Supply, at that time the least desirable and dirtiest job in the hospital. This was before the common use of disposable hospital supplies, such as rubber gloves, hypodermic needles, syringes, and containers. His job was to collect used and dirty items from the hospital wards and clinics, wash them by hand, then sterilize them. The daily workload usually included 500 pairs of rubber gloves, 1000 hypodermic needles and syringes, and 100 or more basins and pans - all containing ordinary hospital refuse and contamination. He was assigned to that job his entire time at the Keesler hospital, over five years.

He never complained about the hazardous health conditions of the job. Neither did he complain about relative rank status of the job although there were people of lesser military rank assigned to better jobs. He faced the job using the concepts of goal orientation and confidence. He devoted himself to be the best he could be from all aspects. He wanted to clean more dirty used rubber gloves than anyone else could. He would clean and sharpen more dirty hypodermic needles than anyone else could. He would also clean more syringes, basins, and pans than anyone else. Then he would ask, "What else needs to be done?"

He completed another year of college by challenge tests. Then he started evening college courses, beginning with the course he feared most: *Speech 101*. He believed that one day he would be justly recognized for his work and self-development goals. Eventually, he was. Three years later a doctor in the audiology department asked if he would like to attend a speech training program to help correct his stuttering problem. The therapy was a six week course at the Forest Glen Speech and Audiology Center, in Maryland.

Not only was another whole new world opened for this young man, two strong guiding principles were also reinforced. Those were: If something is worth having, then you must work for it; and, never let yourself make yourself a loser.

Speech therapy was not an instant cure, nor was it expected to be. Speech therapy for adult stutterers rarely is a total cure. This young man, however, was trained to accept the problem as one that could be handled with the proper mind set, and practice, over a long period of time. There was hope, there was a plan, there was enlightened confidence, and there was steadfast determination.

He went back to real life after completing therapy in an artificial setting that made stuttering seem less abnormal. Now, he had a wife and a young son to support and he knew he couldn't just keep working along, waiting for something to happen. Everything he had achieved so far had occurred by deliberately planning and striving for it. Nothing positive had just randomly happened, simply because he happened to be there. All the positive results had been from positive actions. A good work ethic had not just happened; the college credits had not just happened; the school honor graduate award had not just happened, and the night college courses and other correspondence courses had not just happened. They had resulted from deliberate action that had required much personal determination and effort.

Would these principles help advance his career and his

Reading Opens Learning Doors

economic status to support a family? So far there had been only personal achievements with no tangible or economic rewards. Let's find the answer to the economic question as his true story continues.

It was now 1960, and he was 21 years old. He had just been promoted to airman second class, which raised his monthly pay from $86 to $99. He also received $50 for family housing, which made his total monthly income $149. The outlook for promotions during that time was not good, either. Under conditions that existed at that time, low demand for the military, he knew the next promotion would take two or three more years, and promotion to sergeant no earlier than five to seven years. Should he just wait for those events to take place? He knew the answer was - absolutely not!

Experience had taught him that just to wait for good things to happen would be to wait for deterioration and failure. The only way to advance or to make progress was to do something; *anything*. And he did. His next goal was to complete the biggest project he visualized at that time, to pass the Air Force officers qualification test for Officer Candidate School (OCS.) Of course, he knew it would be impossible to get accepted for that school since he was a marginal student from Mississippi - who stuttered. But, just to pass that qualifying test, passed by so few, would make his qualifications more visible when he was eligible for promotion to sergeant.

The test was a day long battery of aptitude, general knowledge, and military-specific subjects. He passed the first half, graded at noon-time, which permitted him to take the second half in the afternoon. He failed that part. Although disappointed, he knew this was no great tragedy. He was elated. He had done better than most people who had ever taken the test. Furthermore, he now knew the nature and focus of the test and how to prepare for it.

During the year required to retake the test, he prepared to accomplish that goal. He studied general information almanacs, aptitude test preparation guides, English refresher courses, map reading, aerial photography, and aircraft orientation courses. After that year of concentrated preparation he took the test again.

This time tragedy did strike. He failed the first half of the test. He was still an airman second class, and normal promotions looked further away. Although he was disappointed, he looked at his alternatives for career advancement, and again reached the same conclusion: pass that test!

Another year to wait for the test, but also another year to prepare for it: more reading, more studying, more night school, and more correspondence courses. It also required more patience from his wife to accept his dogged determination.

He was prepared again to take that test. It was the third time, after two years of focused effort. Now, however, there was a new obstacle. This was the last test cycle; his last chance. Officer Candidate School was being eliminated to be replaced by a different course, Officer Training School, which required a college degree. Had he studied enough? What was his confidence level? Was he emotionally ready? Was he good enough to pass that test, reserved for only the most qualified? This was not a guessing game or a luck test. Wrong answers on the test were not harmless. They were subtracted from the correct answers. On the positive side, though, he knew he had everything to gain, and nothing to lose. Even if he failed that test, he knew his knowledge, abilities, and perspectives had been enhanced by striving for that important goal.

The test monitor said, "Time." Pencils were placed on the desks and test booklets were passed forward. The test monitor then announced that test scores would be published at 12:30, after lunch. Applicants eligible to take the second half of the test would be notified then; in one hour. Lunch lasted an eternity.

The second half of the test passed quickly. To complete the test there wasn't enough time to read each question carefully and double check each answer. There was only enough time to read a question, make a mark, then move quickly to the next question. He floated into an imaginary dream world when the test monitor said, "You passed!"

What a relief! What a dream come true! He had planned it, he had worked and struggled for it, and he knew he had done it himself.

Reading Opens Learning Doors

No one had simply offered him that success and that feeling of accomplishment on a silver platter. He realized what he needed to do, and he just worked hard enough to do it. He knew that his long-term work record plus the reputation of having passed that test would enhance his possibilities for future promotions.

Soon afterward, he was promoted to a third stripe and sent to a non-commissioned officer (NCO) preparatory school. This month-long course was designed to train airmen for NCO responsibilities. While at that school his regular squadron personnel clerk notified him by telephone that he was not selected for the OCS class. This was not surprising, for he knew he wouldn't be selected for OCS. His goal for taking the test was to help him advance through the NCO ranks.

A day later he received the formal letter that made the announcement. It stated: *You were not selected for the OCS class starting October, 1962. The quota for that class has already been filled. You have been selected for the following class, beginning in January, 1963.* That was the last class of Air Force Officer Candidate School.

While trying to locate the school, on Lackland Air Force Base, in Texas, he visited the information center. The clerk there told him that he, "Would never make it through OCS, for the demands are too high for someone who couldn't talk right."

The six months at OCS, January through June, 1963, was a daily routine of panic and frustration. The course consisted of six hours, daily, of academic classroom subjects in management, communications, military concepts, economics and political geography. The remainder of each day was filled with training usually associated with military activities. This included marching drills, clean-up details, drum and bugle corp practice, and disciplinary fun-and-games by the upper class. These were students in the class that started in October, 1962. They conducted the training other than academics. Study for academic classes was usually after *lights out*, under bed covers, with a flashlight.

Surprisingly to himself, he survived. He was commissioned a

second lieutenant in the U.S. Air Force, June 21, 1963. His wife shared his pride and accomplishment: she pinned the first gold bar insignia onto his collar.

The planning and perseverance rewarded him economically, as well as emotionally. His pay more than doubled in only six months. In December, 1962, his monthly pay was $148. When he was promoted to second lieutenant his pay rose to $335. Combined with the family allowance, his total pay was a little more than $500.

Planning, perseverance, and effort had helped him reach the goal of advancing his career even beyond his expectations. Was this it? Was this the ultimate goal of his career? Of course not. It was only the exciting beginning of new goals guided by higher aspirations. He had learned and reinforced the concept of the power of purposeful planning. He knew that unwavering, goal-directed efforts would produce positive results. He knew it was his responsibility to determine what his future should be. It was his responsibility to plan how to reach those goals. It was also his personal responsibility to make those things happen. He knew he couldn't wait for the *silver platter of success handouts*.

He was twenty-four years old and had been in the Air Force six years. To retire from the Air Force as an officer, in fourteen more years, he knew he must reach the grade of major. Otherwise, he might be reduced to his prior enlisted grade. He also knew that to be competitive for officer promotions he must have a college degree. He had another clear and definite goal: to get that degree.

Japan was his first duty assignment as an officer. There, he completed four on-base college courses: Economics, Philosophy, Conversational Japanese, and English Literature. He was in Japan two years, then was transferred to Saigon, Vietnam.

He was awarded the Air Force Commendation Medal for his service in Japan. He had been promoted to first lieutenant before he transferred, and he was promoted to captain while he was in Vietnam. No courses were available, nor was there time to take college courses, during his year there. He was awarded the Bronze Star for his service in Vietnam.

He returned to the United States, in 1966, and was assigned to Shaw Air Force Base, in Sumter, South Carolina. Shaw AFB had an active base education center, where a counselor advised him that if he completed twelve more semester hours he would be eligible for *Operation Bootstrap*. Bootstrap was a program in which the Air Force, and other military services, assigned its members to a college or university to complete the last thirty semester hours required for a degree.

He completed those twelve hours in one month by taking challenge tests: two in economics and two in accounting. Then he completed the last thirty hours at the University of Nebraska at Omaha, in December, 1971, to earn his degree.

In 1972, he also completed another Air Force program, Air Command and Staff College, by correspondence. He was awarded the Meritorious Service Medal for accomplishments during his six years at Shaw AFB.

He was transferred to Ankara, Turkey, in 1973. There, he entered a new life phase. Instead of being a student, he became a teacher. Instead of withdrawing from public speaking, he taught college courses so military personnel assigned there could continue their college work. He taught four semesters of real estate classes, which were on-base extension courses from the City Colleges of Chicago. These were the only college courses available for students at that time. He had completed a practical real estate course while he was assigned to Shaw AFB, and had taken an academic real estate course, and related courses, while attending the University of Nebraska.

He was promoted to major in the spring of 1974, while still in Turkey. For his performance during that assignment he was also awarded another Meritorious Service Medal (an Oak Leaf added to the first medal.)

In July, 1975, he was transferred to the defense depot at Tracy, California. He had only two more years until he could retire from the Air Force, so it was time to set new goals for a new career. He thought the real estate career offered possibilities, since he had studied and taught real estate for the past four years. Therefore, his new short-term goal was to pass the California real estate broker examination. There were more requirements to take that test. His college degree substituted for the required sales experience, however there were six other college level courses required to qualify for the examination. He completed the required courses by correspondence and challenge tests within three months and got his California real estate broker's license in December, 1977.

In February, 1978, he requested to retire from the Air Force. Two weeks later he received a letter from the Air Force offering to send him to a university for a master's degree. What a difficult decision he faced: to remain in the Air Force, almost guaranteed of career advancements and promotions, or to retire from the Air Force and start a new career at the age of thirty-nine. He chose to start the new career. Why? Because of new challenges.

He retired from the Air Force in April, 1978. During the retirement ceremony he received the Joint Services Commendation Medal for his duty performance at the Defense Depot Tracy.

Were his productive years over? Absolutely not. They had only begun. Although he was not aware of it at that time, his Air Force career was only a learning experience preparing him to become a more positive and contributing part of society.

After his military career he completed another ten-year career in civilian industry. That ten years helped him reconcile concepts and assimilate ideas regarding success and motivation. He learned the same fundamental success principles apply, regardless of the environment. Whether military or civilian, to be successful one must identify a specific goal then actively strive to reach it. A successful person doesn't just wait for success to arrive - to come knocking on the door. It never does. *It must be earned by getting to the end of each row, one row at a time, no matter how long the rows are.*

Where is he now? Presently he's a management and motivation consultant, often presenting personal motivation and success planning speeches to students, and to managers and other leaders in the business world. He is also a writer, specializing in management and personal success planning articles and books.

Hopefully, he will continue to set goals that will improve himself and his happiness, as well as help enhance the careers, attitude, happiness, and security of those who might be influenced by his example and by his writing. He wrote this book for that purpose.

Conclusion

Making good grades in school represents a combination of feelings, aspirations, pressures, and effort. If good grades are a student's goal and the student makes good grades then the student is successful. He or she has accomplished a goal, which is the clear and simple definition of success.

If the student's goal is to graduate from high school, then he or she has accomplished a short-term goal to achieve that long-term goal. If the student's long-term goal is to be successful in life, then the student has set a success pattern by making good grades and by graduating from high school.

Good academic grades give children much more than merely good grades they can show to their parents and other relatives. Good grades also give students pride, esteem, a feeling of higher belonging, and the attitude that success is a natural event. A child who doesn't make good grades has a general success handicap if he or she doesn't have these traits.

Although a student has the basic tool for learning, intelligence, that tool must be influenced and guided properly and positively by teachers and parents. Learning is a team effort, especially during the early years when a child is learning how to learn. Once the child is old enough to read effectively and knows how to learn, the learning process then becomes **habit** and **motivation**.

A child's habits and motivations are most influenced by the child's culture. If the child's home life and friends exemplify failure, despair, laziness, carelessness, weak values, and lack of accepting personal responsibility, the child will be disadvantaged to achieve success. Grades signify only one part of that success attitude.

Parents must set examples of courtesy, caring, responsibility, honesty, respect, and success if they want their children to understand those qualities.

Work, attitude, success, and happiness are qualities and results that go hand-in-hand. Perhaps this concept was explained best by an anonymous Irishman, as reported in Robert Schuller's book, *Possibility Thinking*. He stated:

> *"Take time for work, it is the price of success.*
> *Take time to read, it is the foundation of wisdom.*
> *Take time to be friendly, it is the road to happiness.*
> *Take time to laugh, it is the music of the soul."*

Even within an atmosphere of failure and despair, guided and perpetuated by personal ambitions, cowardice, or ignorance of many politicians and other senior education planners, parents can still help guide their children to success. Those students endowed with good academic skills must be allowed to reach their highest potential. Just as important, students less endowed with academic interest or prowess must not be tossed aside and have their great potential destroyed by elitists' education programs. They must be guided and assisted to achieve the maximum of their potential without destroying their positive dreams and success. Every child is destined for success in some form or avenue, and that success route is not always determined by grades. Their dreams must not be destroyed by forcing them to drop out of school because their interests are elsewhere.

Education must be redesigned to allow success avenues for all children, not just those who are academically, culturally, or socially gifted. Now, our education system is designed backwards: the purpose fits the plan, rather than the plan fitting the purpose for education. This condition is made worse since the purpose for education has not been specified by those creating the plan. The present education plan forces at least a third of our children to drop out. The failure of our country might well result more from the drop-out problem than the grade problem.

Weak grades do not create criminals and perpetual welfare

cases. Currently, the cost to house criminals is greater than the cost of education. How great would be the goal of using that money now wasted to incarcerate criminals to support the motivation needs of students who now lack hope and positive dreams.

As a final thought, with the idea of trying to help sustain our great democratic society, perhaps we should heed the warnings of Thomas Jefferson more seriously. Should we compare his warning with the history of Ancient Greeks who were first to experiment with a form of pure democracy? That experiment failed when conditions evolved similar to evolutions in our democratic society, especially pertaining to welfare reform and education planning.

Are we not, today, seeing the less inspired, the less motivated, and the less successful gaining a greater voice in political decision making. Are we not, today, watching as business leaders who create jobs and more opportunity for individuals' success be denounced and vilified by those whose jealousy and lack of personal achievement distort their interpretation and vision of success?

Are we not, today, watching as the growing masses of less inspired and less motivated have a stronger voice in the call for equal distribution of wealth? Are not many political leaders, today, heeding that voice for personal gain and personal power?

How far do we have to go while we tax the wealthy more to give more to the less-inspired before we move over the dangerous precipice of socialism. Is socially engineering a standard and mediocre education system one of those major steps toward that precipice?

We must never forget that individual success, prosperity, and happiness are earned. They are rewards from personal efforts to be educated and to contribute to our society. They are not things given freely off some silver platter of economic equality. Perhaps one who does not try to earn success rewards would not really understand or appreciate them anyway if they were accepted off that silver platter.

About The Author

Will Clark is an author and lecturer on leadership, work practices, motivation, and study skills. His books include: *Simply Success, The Leadership Handbook, The Power of Positive Education, Who's Blaming Who?, How To Learn,* and *School Bells and Broken Tales.*

As a retired Air Force officer, his experience in leadership and motivation concepts was formed through mixed cultural assignments in several countries. He managed a Japanese workforce for two years, a Vietnamese workforce for one year and a Turkish workforce for two years. He was also an operational readiness inspector and staff evaluator in the Air Force's Tactical Air Command for five years.

He has a degree in Business from the University of Nebraska, and taught college courses to military personnel while he was stationed in Turkey. He also completed Air Force's Air Command and Staff College.

He is the founder of Motivation Basics, a firm that provides leadership, workplace, productivity and study skills training. He is also the founder of a civic organization, Friends of Education, that promotes education projects and assists needy causes. He is a past president of the Southaven, Mississippi, Optimist Club, and a past Optimist lieutenant governor for his Optimist area.

Appendix A

Index of Parenting Skills

		Page
1.	Be a Learning Partner	84
2.	Focus on Effort - Not Grades	87
3.	Keep Communications Open	89
4.	Schedule Talk Time	92
5.	Understand the Learning Process	94
6.	Know the Teacher	96
7.	Become Involved	97
8.	Teach Positive Self-Esteem	98
9.	Give Books as Gifts	100
10.	Introduce the Child to the Library	102

Appendix B

Index of Student Learning Skills

	Page
1. Choose a good study area	104
2. Prepare the study area	105
3. Set a routine study time	107
4. The parent must participate	109
5. Get enough exercise	110
6. Get enough sleep	112
7. Don't be guided by peer pressure	114
8. Learn to listen	116
9. Learn to take notes	118
10. Learn to outline or hi-lite	120
11. Use flash cards	122
12. Improve reading skills	124
13. Use a timer while studying	126
14. Create a good environment	127
15. Choose successful friends	129
16. Set realistic goals	131
17. Trust yourself and like yourself	133
18. Don't be afraid to ask for help	135
19. Learn how to take tests	137
20. Reward yourself	140

Bibliography

Ken Auletta, *The Underclass* (Vintage Books, New York, 1982)
Bernard Berelson and Gary Steiner, *Human Behavior* (Harcourt, Brace & World, 1964)
J. Jay Braun, Darwyn E. Linder, Isaac Asimov, *Psychology Today* (Random House, New York, NY, 1979)
Frederick Herzberg, et. el., *The Motivation to Work* (Wiley and Sons, New York, NY, 1959).
J.N. Hook, *Testmanship* (Barnes & Noble, New York, NY, 1967)
Michael B. Katz, *In The Shadow of the Poorhouse* (Basic Books, Inc., Publishers, New York, 1986)
Donald M. Levine and Mary Jo Bane, *The Inequality Controversy: Schooling and Distributive Justice* (Basic Books, Inc., Publishers, New York, 1975)
Harry Maddox, *How To Study* (Fawcett Publications, Inc., Greenwich, CT, 1963)
Abraham H. Maslow, *Motivation and Personality* (Harper and Rowe, New York, NY, 1954)
Clifford T. Morgan, *Introduction to Psychology* (McGraw-Hill Book Co., Inc., 1956)
Ivor Morrish, *Disciplines of Education* (George Allen & Unwin Ltd., Great Britain, 1967)
Albert J. Pautler, et. el., *Career Education* (MSS Information Corporation, 1973)
Bertrand Russell, *Authority and the Individual* (Beacon Press, Boston, 1949)
Samuel Smith, *Read it Right and Remember What You Read* (Barnes & Noble, New York, NY, 1970)
James D. Weinland, *How to Improve Your Memory* (Barnes & Noble, New York, NY, 1968)

Reading Opens Learning Doors

Made in the USA
Columbia, SC
02 October 2023